Language and Narratives *in* Counseling and Psychotherapy

Scott T. Meier, PhD, is Professor in the Department of Counseling, School, and Educational Psychology, University at Buffalo. He is a licensed psychologist who received his PhD in Counseling Psychology from Southern Illinois University, Carbondale, in 1984. Meier's major research and teaching areas focus on psychological measurement (particularly outcome assessment), research methods (particularly program evaluation), and counseling skills (particularly the integration of case conceptualization and assessment with intervention). He is a member of the American Evaluation Association, the Association for Psychological Science, and the Association for Behavioral and Cognitive Therapies. Meier is the author or co-author of five books (including *Measuring Change in Counseling and Psychotherapy* and *Elements of Counseling*) and has published in the *American Psychologist, Canadian Journal of School Psychology, Journal of Counseling Psychology, Measurement and Evaluation in Counseling and Development*, and the *American Journal of Evaluation*.

Language and Narratives
in
Counseling and Psychotherapy

Scott T. Meier, PhD

Springer Publishing Company, LLC
11 West 42nd Street
New York, NY 10036
www.springerpub.com

Acquisitions Editor: Nancy Hale
Composition: Techset

ISBN: 978-0-8261-0896-8
E-book ISBN: 978-0-8261-0897-5

12 13 14/ 5 4 3 2 1

CIP data is available from the Library of Congress

Printed in the United States of America by Gasch Printing

Contents

Preface

The first goal of this book is to make principles related to language and narratives in counseling and psychotherapy explicit and easier to learn. While acknowledging the social constructivist philosophy underlying many narrative therapies, this book employs a more pragmatic approach for conceptualizing and applying language-related principles. The book emphasizes brevity, clarity of presentation, and multiple examples. The description of principles and guidelines includes a general introduction, one or more examples, and then an elaboration or deepening of the idea, often including relevant research that provides an empirical basis for the principle or practice. Each chapter begins with basic ideas and builds to more complex principles, and each chapter's set of principles can be employed as a checklist of competencies for assessing students or self.

The book integrates diverse approaches and borrows from other works, in part because elements of language and narratives are integral to all schools of psychotherapy. I present a realignment of existing psychotherapy constructs and principles into a model based on narrative and language ideas. Using narrative therapies (NTs) as an explanatory framework, it is now possible to piece together the basic elements of effective interventions across psychotherapy schools; a brief list of approaches employed in this integration includes behavioral, cognitive behavioral, object relations, Gestalt, family therapy, grief, psychodynamic, interpersonal, and client-centered therapies. Research in clinical and basic science domains, including emotion science, word usage, emotions, meaning-making, and narratives (Angus & McLeod, 2004; Campbell-Sills & Barlow, 2007; Mergenthaler, 1996; Moses & Barlow, 2006; Tausczik & Pennebaker, 2010), has provided important clues about what makes effective psychotherapy. The unification offered by narrative therapy concepts also provides guidance about what should be assessed to gauge client progress in counseling and psychotherapy.

This work can be considered a bookend to the *Elements of Counseling* (Meier & Davis, 2011). The seven editions of *Elements* emphasize pre-intervention steps and stages in psychotherapy, focusing on listening skills, relationship building, counseling process, and self-exploration. Therapist-client conversations differ from ordinary conservations on several dimensions, the primary reason being that therapeutic exchanges are aimed at helping the client change (Meier & Davis, 2011). By listening well, the therapist helps the client attend to what she or he is experiencing, feeling, and doing. Listening well is a major component in making a conversation therapeutic, building relationships even between individuals of different backgrounds (Bruner, 2004), and sets the stage for subsequent therapeutic interventions.

With the preintervention foundation laid, this book complements *Elements* by using narratives and language as its organizing framework to summarize key procedures and options in the intervention phase of psychotherapy. As Huler (2004, p. 91) wrote, "Language is technology. It's a tool to accomplish a task." A second goal of this book, consequently, is to convey the idea that a narrative model can be usefully construed as an umbrella theory, organizing a variety of concepts that specify what effective therapists do with psychotherapy clients. As one of the book's reviewers wrote, the text aims to provide "a comprehensive overview that links a popular theory and set of techniques to the broad array of theoretical orientations students become familiar with." Coupled with extensive training through clinical experience, role-plays, professional supervision, and learning of relevant theory and research results, students can master best practices and have those skills become automatic.

This book is intended primarily for use in advanced psychotherapy and practicum courses in counseling, psychology, and social work, including programs in mental health counseling, marriage and family counseling, rehabilitation counseling, school counseling, counseling psychology, clinical psychology, school psychology, and social work. The clinical modality typically referenced in the book is individual therapy with adults in an outpatient setting, but many of the principles will be applicable to other patient populations and settings. In addition, the distillation of key principles related to narratives and language use in psychotherapy ensures that the content will be accessible to instructors and students across theoretical orientations.

Experienced therapists who wish to learn about how to employ narrative approaches in their own practices will also find the book useful. For experienced therapists with a sense of the importance of language in therapy, this book may function as a heuristic device for thinking about psychotherapy with particular clients. That is, the principles and descriptions in the book may spark additional ideas about how to process and intervene with clients. Experienced therapists are likely to recognize many of these principles because of their extensive catalog of metaphors and stories they have amassed over years of clinical work.

One of the key assumptions of narrative approaches to psychotherapy is that everyone employs language in both common and idiosyncratic ways. When we describe our selves and relations with various environments, particularly social environments, our language has enough commonality so that others can understand, at some level, the intended meaning. At the same time, everyone's language use is unique to some degree, and consequently reflective of our psychological status and learning history, as influenced by family, culture, age, gender, religion, and so forth. So let me acknowledge that many readers would substitute different word choices at places in this book. Some readers, for example, might cringe at the use of the term "client" instead of "patient," or the use of "psychotherapy" instead of "counseling." Everyone has preferences for language use, and this includes the use of words to describe the meaning of professional, scientific, and clinical terms. In a sense, this is an unfinished, organic book because of the reader's (your) ability to change and modify its content and meanings. If you have ideas about how to improve this book's presentation, please email me at the address on page xi.

From a narrative perspective, the principles described in this book can be revised, rewritten, and improved *ad infinitum*. Similarly, no end exists to the number of language-related principles that could be created, based on the writer's profession, history, culture, and time period, for example. I am confident, however, that the principles described in this book reflect some universal aspects of current psychological knowledge and perspectives. While the book draws on NT approaches, this is not a book about NT per se. Instead, I focus on the central, but often implicit, role of narratives and language in counseling and psychotherapy. Michael White is often credited as the founder of NT, but even a brief review of the literature reveals that NT has not coalesced into a single, cohesive approach. As McLeod (1997, p. x) observed:

> There is no "narrative therapy," there is no one way of doing this. To present "narrative therapy" as a new brand-name product in the therapeutic marketplace (with accompanying training manual) is to misunderstand what this is all about.

So the practice in the remainder of this book will be to refer to NTs, not to a single NT.

Chapter 1 provides an introduction, rationale, and primer for the key ideas in the book, including the philosophical underpinnings of NTs in social constructivism. The relations between client narratives and affect, cognition, and behavior are outlined in preparation for the detailed descriptions of narrative principles in the next three chapters. The use of client affect, cognition, and behavior as organizing concepts follows traditional conceptualizations in psychotherapy, but the narrative perspective on these three domains makes it clear that considerable linkage naturally occurs. Instructors may wish to rearrange principles in these chapters to fit their teaching strategies or add other domains (e.g., interpersonal elements) to their presentations. Chapters 2 through 4 are sufficiently interconnected that readers may wish to read across chapters at times to see how affective, cognitive, and behavioral interventions can interact to change client narratives.

Chapter 2 addresses narratives and emotion, noting that affective language, particularly language about negative affect (NA), frequently marks key content in client narratives; this chapter describes how to help clients process and experience strong affect, a theoretically and empirically based key element for client change. Chapter 3 focuses on the client's cognitions and meaning-making in the therapy process. This includes how clients interpret the events and situations in their lives, what themes recur over time, and how to recognize ill-formed narratives. The chapter concludes with a description of the process of shifting between affective processing and meaning-making, which research suggests is a key sequence in effective psychotherapy. Chapter 4 describes the role of client behaviors and activities from a narrative perspective. While most narrative therapists see behavior therapy as philosophically opposite, client behaviors have the capacity to influence self-descriptions. Narratives can be deepened and changed through a variety of activities, including creating therapeutic documents, role-plays, homework, and data-based feedback.

Chapter 5 identifies major obstacles, from a narrative perspective, to therapeutic progress introduced by clients and therapists. For clients, this can involve being unaware of or resistant to experiencing and expressing strong NA and associated situations. Therapist obstacles include difficulties tolerating clients' affective discomfort and hypothesis confirmation bias. Chapter 6 presents major assessment issues in psychotherapy and then outlines methods for assessing narrative characteristics as well as the major domains of affect (NA), cognitions (recurring themes, self-efficacy), and behavior (verbal behaviors, self-monitoring). I present the case for NT as a unifying theory in Chapters 1 and 7. In Chapter 1, I describe the benefits of employing NTs as a unifying metaphor, while in Chapter 7 more depth is provided about the problems of disunity and the prospects for providing an integrative theoretical framework via narrative concepts.

My interest in language is long-standing: I was one of those peculiar students who enjoyed leafing through the pages of a dictionary to explore new words. My interest continued in college as a dual major in English and Psychology and while I worked for several years as a newspaper reporter. In graduate school I became interested in the problem of disunity in psychological theory, research, and practice (Meier, 1987), and it was not until almost 25 years later, when I began to read accounts of NTs, did I see a strong potential solution appear. I hope this book contributes to the integrationist movement in psychotherapy, counseling, and psychology.

Thanks to University at Buffalo (UB) students Gwen Lander and Dr. Wendy Guyker for permission to use their tables of client information in the book. Thanks also to Nancy Hale for important feedback as she shepherded this project through the proposal and review stages and to UB graduate assistant Danielle Gissinger for useful conversations about narratives. Thanks also to Dr. Edith Jacobs of Linwood Psychotherapy Services for comments on an early draft. Finally, I would like to acknowledge the helpful comments of the book's reviewers on the initial proposal: Christian Conte (University of Nevada-Reno), Jerry Gale (University of Georgia), Douglas Guiffrida (University of Rochester), and Rita Sommers-Flanagan (University of Montana).

Scott T. Meier, PhD
stmeier@buffalo.edu

One

Introduction and Foundations

Narrative therapies (NTs) encompass a range of approaches that emphasize the importance of language and stories in counseling and psychotherapy (Angus & McLeod, 2004). NTs emphasize that clients tell stories in therapy that can be useful in assessing and helping clients. As Tausczik and Pennebaker (2010, p. 25) described,

> Language is the most common and reliable way for people to translate their thoughts and emotions into a form that others can understand. Words and language, then, are the very stuff of psychology and communication.

White (2004, p. 38) described people as "active, impassioned meaning makers in search of plausible stories." Similarly, Madigan (2011, p. 33) wrote that a key idea of NTs is "that it is the stories people tell and hold about their lives that determine the meaning they give to their lives." We make sense of our life experiences through stories, which can be considered informal theories that map personal experiences for later recall and guidance about current and future situations. For most people, stories are interesting and easy ways to remember important information (Linehan, 1993).

Counseling and psychotherapy have been referred to as talk therapies because clients and therapists employ language to communicate and provide therapy. One of the important ways in which we can distinguish the quality of helping professionals is by how well they are able to listen to client narratives and communicate that listening to clients. And almost all therapies depend heavily upon language to deliver their therapeutic interventions. Even psychiatrists who rely primarily on psychopharmacological interventions depend on (a) the patient's use of language to describe symptoms and clinical progress and (b) their own language and listening skills to develop a relationship with patients and persuade patients to adhere to the prescribed regimen.

THEORETICAL AND PHILOSOPHICAL FOUNDATIONS OF NTs

Proponents of NTs often emphasize the philosophical underpinnings of narrative approaches. *Logical positivism* is a philosophical school based on the concept that an objective reality exists (Glesne, 2011). In contrast, NTs build on a *constructivist* approach that proposes that an apparent reality is a social construction that does not exist in any meaningful way independent of social interactions. *Critical theory* recognizes the role of different ideologies (e.g., political, cultural, economic) in distorting apparent reality, particularly for and about oppressed groups; as Glesne (2011, p. 10) summarizes, "critical theory researchers see research as a political act because it not only relies on value systems, but challenges value systems." Finally, *postmodernism* argues that no universal truths exist and that researchers must be grounded by their historical and local *contexts*.

Thus, postmodernism focuses on the ideas that apparent reality is socially constructed through language, and organized and maintained with narratives (Freedman & Combs, 1996). As Gergen (2001, p. 805) observed, "we use language to report on the nature of the world as we see it." Consider the simple idea of a "chair." As shown in Figure 1.1, the concept of "chair" can represent very different objects. Wallerstein (1982, p. 10) wrote that words "are not necessarily what they seem, able to be taken at face value with one unvarying definitional truth value, but rather are varyingly transparent or obscure bridges between surface manifest meaning and underlying latent meaning." Similarly, the idea of "stairs" will have different meanings and *implications* for able-bodied persons than for individuals with arthritis, on crutches, or in a wheelchair. As a subject of interest in *semiotics*, language is a sign system that represents something else (Chandler, 2007). Thus, language forms a useful, but imperfect, method for representing and communicating human experience and perception (D. Gissinger, personal communication, January 24, 2011).

These postmodern ideas will be appealing to therapists whose everyday dealings with clients and patients demonstrate the social construction of apparent reality, particularly in interpersonal relationships, and the central role of language and narratives in that construction. Anyone who has functioned as a psychotherapist, observing the seemingly infinite ways different individuals perceive and describe similar life situations, will have at least an intuitive understanding of social constructivism. Narrative therapists help clients see that their worlds are constructed through language and cultural practice and that clients can subsequently deconstruct and reconstruct their assumptions and perceptions. As Stiles (2001) indicated, the meaning of words can change across time and people. Discussing the work of Milton Erickson, Freedman and Combs (1996) noted

FIGURE 1.1 *'Chair' can represent very different objects.*

that "people can continually and actively re-author their lives ... there are many possible experiential realities" (p. 11) and that "our experiential realities are constituted by language" (p. 12).

NARRATIVES AND PSYCHOTHERAPY

For the purposes of psychotherapy, a client's narratives describe that person's psychological realities. Greenberg and Angus (2004, p. 333) cited Damasio (1999) as arguing that "human beings essentially live and breathe in a world that is ordered and experienced as an unfolding story in time." Bruner (2004, p. 13) maintained that narrative is "irresistible as a way of making sense of human interaction" and that even our ideas of self depend upon narratives: "The construction of a selfhood ... cannot proceed without a capacity to narrate" (Bruner, 2004, p. 13). Individuals with a neurological disorder called *dysnarrativia,* a severe impairment in the ability to tell or understand stories, have disruptions in affect and memory to the extent that "selfhood virtually vanishes" (Bruner, 2004, p. 13).

Anderson (2004) proposed that stories are social enterprises, co-constructed by two or more people. It follows that a client's telling of stories to a skilled listener typically leads to rapport building and bonding between client and therapist. In addition, the therapist may influence the type of stories that the client tells to the therapist; the specific questions that a therapist asks a client, for example, may influence the answers the client provides. Anyone who doubts that a particular therapist–client dyad influences the therapeutic narratives should view the differential clinical pictures provided in the well-known training videos with the client Gloria, working with Carl Rogers, Fritz Perls, and Albert Ellis (Shostrum, 1966); segments of these videos can be seen, for example, on YouTube. This can also involve questions of social power for narrative therapists, who pay attention to whose stories have credibility in a particular situation, whose stories should be listened to, and who gets to tell stories—issues of particular importance in families and work organizations, for example. Client stories are face valid, that is, they have intrinsic value, and narrative therapists assume that client stories reflect some meaningful aspect of that person.

Stories obviously have content, but out of the vast amount of information provided by a client, what should a therapist pay attention to? From a language and narrative perspective, several characteristics are important. Strong affect marks key elements of stories, demarcating material that should be explored in great detail. Client stories are presumed to be incomplete in the sense that people may omit important material from actual events when they store information in narratives; clients may have difficulty discussing important content because of its association with strong negative affect. Recurrent or repeated themes also suggest material that will benefit from therapeutic attention. Clients' *self-descriptions* about self-agency (i.e., personal competence for influencing people, events, and tasks) are often central to therapeutic progress; strategies to change client behavior and consequently influence self-descriptions then become a focus of therapeutic intervention (Bandura, 1977, 1997). These characteristics are described in further detail in the remainder of this chapter and form the core of important content in the remaining chapters in this book.

AFFECTIVE ELEMENTS OF NARRATIVES

Barrett (2006, p. 48) suggested that basic affect "is a neurophysiological barometer of the individual's relation to an environment at a given point in time, and self-reported feelings are the barometer readings." Perls, Hefferline, and Goodman (1951, cited in Greenberg, Korman, & Paivio, 2001, p. 499) defined emotion "as people's direct evaluative experience of the field that provides knowledge of the objects appropriate to their needs."

Emotion researchers maintain that affect is central to human functioning (Izard, 2007; Persons, 1991): Feelings inform individuals about their status in an actual or perceived *environment* (Campbell-Sills & Barlow, 2007), and these signals function as powerful motivators for human activity (Frijda, 1986).

Emotion researchers have found the constructs of *positive affect* (PA) and *negative affect* (NA) to be useful descriptions of human emotional characteristics found across cultures. PA refers to emotions experienced as pleasant states (such as happiness), while NA are emotions experienced as unpleasant or aversive (such as sadness; Barrett, 2006). Some researchers characterize emotions as either *universal basic emotions* (BEs), such as PA and NA, or more complex *emotion schemas* (ESs), in which individuals think idiosyncratically about their emotions as well as the situations that elicited those emotions (Izard, 2007). Izard (2007) suggested that in comparison with BEs, ESs are greater in frequency and longer in duration. For example, an individual with a fear of flying may, while actually flying on an airplane, occasionally experience the basic emotion of fear. This individual, however, will more frequently feel slightly to moderately anxious while thinking about an upcoming trip that involves flying (i.e., an emotion schema in which anxiety is elicited when thinking about flying).

Mergenthaler (1996, p. 1306) maintains that emotion is "a central aspect of many or all psychotherapies." Greenberg and Angus (2004, p. 333) similarly emphasize the centrality of emotion in narratives, suggesting that stories themselves are shaped by the emotional themes present and that emotions are the "primary associative connection" of story elements. From a psychotherapy perspective, the key elements of client stories will be marked by affect, particularly NA. Because emotional reactions to an event increase the likelihood that an event will be remembered (Payne & Kensinger, 2010), what stories are important to clients and what stories clients remember to tell their therapists should be influenced by the type and intensity of affect associated with those stories. Similarly, what clients remember from psychotherapy, both in session and outside of session, should be strongly influenced by the affect associated with client–psychotherapist dialogs and events. An emotion focus also has implications for progress and outcome *assessment*: As clients' problems resolve, client reports of NA should decrease in frequency and intensity (Meier & Vermeersch, 2007).

Given this background, NA has two important functions that should be examined in the context of counseling and psychotherapy. First, NA is the usual concomitant emotion for all human problems; an important loss, for example, will be accompanied by sadness; an impending threat, by *anxiety*. Second, individuals may think about their NA; for some individuals in some situations, affective states have implications. Thus, a person who experienced strong anxiety when speaking in public during a class or work presentation may begin to ruminate about that anxiety. Essentially, this person now has two problems: The task of speaking publicly in a competent manner, and the task of coping with worrying about that task. Depending upon the individual, learning the skills to perform as a competent public speaker may or may not lead to a decrease in worrying. Thus, while some general principles can be proposed about the role of NA in human functioning and in psychotherapy progress, the *idiographic* nature of human functioning and response to psychotherapy remains equally important.

COGNITIVE ELEMENTS OF NARRATIVES

The client's self-descriptions, recurring themes, incomplete life stories, distorted (from others' perspective) beliefs, polarities, and perceived contexts are all examples of important therapeutic content and client cognitions. Strong affect also signals important content, and the weaving between exploration of affect and related content—sometimes unique to the particular client/therapist dyad—is a key therapeutic process.

From a cognitive perspective, stories and narratives fulfill several roles relevant to psychological functioning (Meier, 2008a). Narratives allow storage in memory of large amounts of information relevant to personal goals, ways to attain those goals, and the individual's relevant competencies. The client's language and stories are likely to repeat central themes; a depressed individual, for example, may narrate stories which essentially indicate "I am helpless to influence important life events." Narratives also provide a mechanism for decision-making (Dimaggio & Semerari, 2004); if a current situation fits a previous narrative, guidelines for behavior implicitly follow. Finally, stories may be used to extract key elements and organize the complex information contained in social interactions and experiences (Boothe & Von Wyl, 2004).

Recall that White (2004, p. 38) suggested that humans are "active, impassioned meaning makers in search of plausible stories." Narratives help us make sense of the events in our lives and remember key lessons for future application. Narrative therapists and their clients find and create meaning in client stories, with the goals of helping clients understand themselves and change some aspect of their lives. *Deconstruction*, for example, is the process in which therapists help clients become aware of the dominant story that guides their lives and to question its themes so that the story becomes just one possible view of the self. Other life events become more fully incorporated into the story and the client becomes a more active protagonist in the story. The student who reports that she "must get an A on a particular test"—an *irrational belief*, in Ellis's Rational Emotive Behavior Therapy (REBT; 1998) lexicon—may tell stories of other tests in which she felt pressure to perform well. However, she may also recall situations in which she performed poorly and no catastrophic consequences resulted as well as instances when she felt relaxed while performing. Narrative therapists explore such events in an attempt to integrate an expanded account into the client's dominant plot.

BEHAVIORAL ELEMENTS OF NARRATIVES

Sometimes underemphasized in NT discussions, behavior is important in client narratives for several reasons. First, narratives can be considered blueprints for action in particular contexts. In client narratives, the key elements are behaviors, broadly construed, that the client or others perform, often in relationships; clients tell stories about an argument with a spouse, or how they work or study too many hours. The emotions and meanings described in client narratives also take place in particular situations, contexts, and environments. Thus, therapists may be able to influence client narratives and self-descriptions through knowledge of and intervention with specific behaviors, situations, and environments.

To the extent that a change in a client's self-description is important to therapeutic outcome, behavior can play a key role. One of the dangers of narrative approaches is for the client and therapist to believe that changing a narrative in session is sufficient to produce changes that generalize to other settings. But behavior in the world outside the session, with the key people in the client's narratives, may produce much more credible information. Affective processing and *meaning-making* may be insufficient for change to take hold outside the therapy session and be maintained over time. *Homework, therapeutic documents, role-plays, clinically relevant feedback,* and *exposure* to feared situations may be necessary to convince clients of their new self-descriptions and to cement those descriptions as credible for future use. If narratives are the scripts of clients' lives, then behaviors are the acting of those scripts in the client's life.

A NARRATIVE-BASED THEORY OF CHANGE

As shown in Figure 1.2, a narrative-based theory of change for individuals in counseling and psychotherapy typically involves multiple, converging pathways of affective, cognitive, and behavioral effort (Anderson, 2004). Greenberg and Angus (2004, p. 346) summarized the process:

> In the process of articulating and reflecting on life experiences in psychotherapy, personal narratives become deeper—fused with

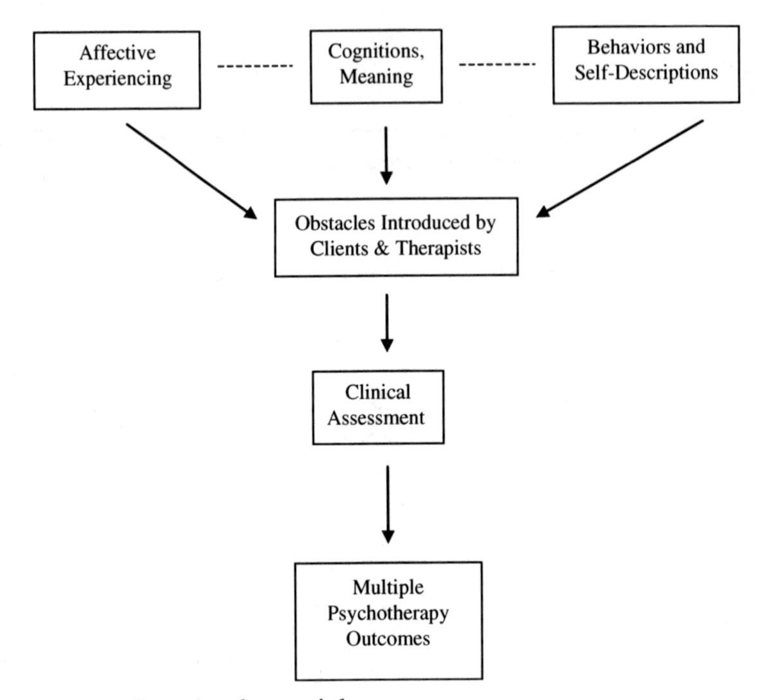

FIGURE 1.2 *Narrative theory of change.*
Note: *Clients process affect, search for meaning, and try out new behaviors and self-descriptions. The therapy process can be complicated by obstacles presented by clients and therapists. Assessment of all of these domains can provide useful feedback during therapy. For most clients, this complex process typically results in multiple outcomes.*

> emotional meaning and significance—as well as larger—taking more information into account ... The constantly evolving self operates as a synthesizing process, creating and being created anew in each moment and situation.

Individuals recall, relate, and generate one or more stories that contain people, events, and situations with associated emotional elements. Much of the initial stage of psychotherapy involves identifying those emotions and the extent to which the client can tolerate their expression and experience. All these processes take place in social contexts; in psychotherapy, these contexts include the client–therapist relationship and relationships among clients in group, family, and couple settings.

Identifying emotions and the accompanying content about persons and events creates an agenda for processing and resolving the individual's psychological difficulties in psychotherapy. Samoilov and Goldfried (2000,

p. 382) indicate that emotional arousal lays the foundation for "reorganization of underlying emotional themes, assimilation of new information, and formation of new implicit meaning structures." Next, individuals create meaning in their psychotherapy-related stories to solve or resolve the distress-causing situation. Often, a change in self-description around personal agency is part of this process and here a focus on behavior change can be beneficial. Formal clinical assessment can provide feedback to therapist and client about the degree and direction of therapeutic progress. This clinical process is seldom straightforward, however, as many individuals struggle with obstacles to processing of content associated with strong emotion as well as changing problem-related behaviors.

Empirical support for NTs and these specific change components has been found in studies employing a range of methodologies (e.g., Silver, Williams, Worthington, & Phillips, 1998; Vromans & Schweitzer, 2010; Weber, Davis, & McPhie, 2006). Vromans and Schweitzer (2010), for example, examined *depression* and interpersonal outcomes for 47 adults with major depression who received *manualized narrative therapy* (i.e., where therapists had a written set of narrative-related procedures to employ in a particular sequence). Results indicated significant improvement for both depressive symptoms and interpersonal functioning. Researchers have also found that writing about emotional upheavals can positively affect psychological and physical health (Pennebaker, Mehl, & Niederhoffer, 2003). In these studies, individuals typically write about an emotionally disturbing topic for 15–30 minutes per day over a 3- to 5-day period. Such writing can not only lead to long-term improvements but also produce short-term increases in emotional distress (Smyth, 1998). Other research has found that facilitating *emotional processing* and *verbalization of affect* is associated with positive outcomes (Diener, Hilsenroth, & Weinberger, 2007).

OBSTACLES TO CHANGE

From a narrative and language perspective, a variety of factors can present obstacles to change. Narrative therapists maintain that aspects of clients' lived experiences have been *excluded* from narratives. For example, clients may be unaware of strong NA, or even when they are aware of such feelings, clients may be unwilling to talk about them. Dealing with difficult emotions is a key element of many different therapeutic approaches (e.g., Linehan, 1993; Samoilov & Goldfried, 2000; Teyber & McClure, 2011). Clients may be very reluctant to share strong feelings because they do not expect to improve in psychotherapy, may be ashamed to reveal secrets or admit failure and thus expect to be critically judged, or fear losing control (Teyber & McClure, 2011).

Similarly, strong affect can be a problem for therapists. Research indicates that even experienced psychotherapists may avoid addressing clients' sensitive and strong NA (Hill & O'Brien, 1999; Teyber & McClure, 2011). Therapists' ability to be open and accepting of clients' feelings may be influenced by their own emotional states, their inexperience with strong NA (particularly for therapists in training), and their feelings of responsibility for causing or resolving clients' strong emotions. While emotional issues may be a central source of therapist-provided obstacles, therapists can also hinder the client's sharing of therapeutic material through such acts as talking too much, giving advice, and premature problem solving (Meier & Davis, 2011).

NARRATIVES AND CLINICAL ASSESSMENT

Mental health providers have demonstrated considerable creativity and expertise for creating and delivering psychosocial interventions. On the other hand, the field's major weakness is the lack of suitable instruments for providing targeted feedback about the usefulness of psychotherapeutic interventions across sessions. For both practice and research, this is a major sticking point for progress in the field. All scientific domains must grapple with the measurement problem in their initial development. Historically, new measurement techniques have been found to drive scientific development (Cone & Foster, 1991; Forbes & Dijksterhuis, 1963). Tryon (1991, p. 1) observed that "the history of science is largely coextensive with the history of measurement," while Cone (1988, p. 42) wrote that "it is certainly beyond argument that the building of all science rests on a foundation of accurate measurement."

Given the current preliminary status of measurement theory in psychotherapy, it should not be surprising that many therapists do not employ formal measurement devices in practice, much less instruments specifically designed for assessing progress and outcome. Sapyta, Riember, and Bickman (2005, p. 147; cf. Clement, 1994, 1999) noted that "therapists are trained, are supervised, and practice in the absence of information about client treatment response from objective sources." Equally problematic, many therapists and researchers appear quite confident about their abilities to create, evaluate, or employ data from clinical assessments and professional judgments despite evidence to the contrary (Ziskin, 1995). Gray and Lambert's (2001) review of research on clinicians' judgment of client progress, for example, concluded that "clinicians are not effective in gauging patient response to treatment, especially in early treatment sessions" (p. 26).

Clinical assessment related to narratives focuses on client story characteristics and client affect, cognitions, and behaviors. Story characteristics refer to the particular content of client narratives as well as the form of those stories (e.g., organization and coherence of the narrative). Affective measures focus on scales for NA and affective experience, while cognitive measures assess clinical themes and content, including changes in narrative themes over time. Behavioral measures include self-monitoring of client behaviors, including verbal and nonverbal behaviors, and self-efficacy expectations related to clients' perceived ability to perform desired behaviors.

NARRATIVES AS A UNIFYING METAPHOR IN COUNSELING AND PSYCHOTHERAPY

Some theorists treat NTs as a distinct type of psychotherapy. Distinct therapeutic approaches have explanatory principles, a particular vocabulary, specific techniques associated with them, and a small nucleus of experts who disseminate the knowledge associated with the approach through workshops, publications, videos, and other media (Corsini & Wedding, 2007). New approaches typically critique previous approaches as a rationale for the new method. Madigan (2011, p. 14), for example, wrote about David Epston, a colleague of White, that "his creativity seemed to stem from his first realization that ongoing behavioral and structural approaches to treating problems encountered by children and adults were largely ineffective."

Counseling and psychotherapy approaches also can be characterized as occurring within distinct time frames or histories. Carlson and Englar-Carlson (2011), for example, portrayed distinct schools of psychotherapy as arriving in waves: The first wave was psychodynamic theories, followed by learning, humanistic, feminist/multicultural, and now, postmodern and constructivist theories. This *metaphor* of *waves* is useful in that it implies that the dominant psychotherapy theories change and evolve, signifying progress over time. But the wave metaphor also implies that there is no end to the progression of psychotherapy theories. To external observers, it may appear that the field has no center, but is essentially a series of fads that excites a core of disciples, many of whom eventually lose interest and get swept into the next wave.

Instead of considering NTs as one more wave, another metaphor that may be useful is that of a large tree. Consider narratives and language as the trunk of the tree, from which all branches develop. The tree may continue to grow over time, adding new branches; even as older branches age and eventually fall off, there is no end to the possibility of new schools and approaches to psychotherapy. Adopting a narrative framework as an organizing theory does not preclude therapists or researchers from adopting or exploring branches on the tree. Yet all branches depend upon the core: Language and narrative infuse all psychotherapeutic approaches, and appreciation of this view can lead the practitioner of any approach to consider language-inspired methods for improving the delivery and effectiveness of a particular approach. The core, while growing, essentially remains the same: Any approach that we label as counseling and psychotherapy will depend heavily upon narratives and language in the communication between therapist and client, whether the client modality is individual, couple, family, or group.

SUMMARY AND IMPLICATIONS

Contemporary psychotherapeutic approaches are talk therapies that rely on language to deliver their therapeutic impact. NTs offer a unifying perspective that applies to most clients, therapists, and schools of counseling and psychotherapy, providing ideas about how to help clients tell their stories, what to listen for, and how to employ that material in a therapeutic manner. In particular, narrative therapists notice the presence or absence of certain elements in stories to be helpful with particular clients.

For most clients, therapy begins with the client telling an initial story that typically contains a presenting problem. As described in Chapter 2, the therapist helps the client to elaborate on and deepen that story, with considerable attention focused on exploring elements with emotional content. Chapter 3 describes how once the affective story elements have been sufficiently explored and elaborated, the focus turns to meaning-making and subsequent resolution of the problem(s). As described in Chapter 4, a change in client self-description is facilitated by behavioral interventions. Numerous examples of how therapists from affective/experiencing, cognitive, and behavioral traditions employ language and narratives in their work are provided in Chapters 2 through 4. Skilled therapists learn how to help clients weave connections between affect, cognitions, and behaviors in personal narratives.

While client- and therapist-produced obstacles to therapeutic progress are described in Chapter 5, progress in psychotherapy can be facilitated by the use of appropriate clinical assessments, as described in Chapter 6. Chapter 7 summarizes key propositions of the book and further describes how a narrative approach may function usefully as a unifying model for psychotherapy theory and practice.

Two

Affective Elements of Narratives

Painful feelings bring clients into therapy, and therapists' recognition of and work with such feelings is often an important element of client change (Teyber & McClure, 2011). Much of the information in this chapter corresponds roughly to what psychotherapists term the *exploration phase* of therapy (Egan, 2001; Ivey, 2002) or storytelling of autobiographical events (Hardtke & Angus, 2004). The goal of such exploration is to help clients talk more deeply and specifically about the emotionally laden content of their clinically relevant stories (Greenberg, 2002).

Two important types of negative emotions that clients frequently express are *depression* and *anxiety*, common reactions to stressful life events (Carter, 2007). While a variety of definitions exist for both constructs, depression refers to feelings of sadness triggered by past events such as a significant loss. In contrast, anxiety is future focused; Bandura (1977, p. 137) defined anxiety as "a state of anticipatory apprehension over possible deleterious happenings." Depression and anxiety often co-occur (McLaughlin, Borkovec, & Sibrava, 2007; Moses & Barlow, 2006) and accompany many psychological problems ranging from obsessive–compulsive disorder (Abramowitz, 2002) to kleptomania (McElroy, Hudson, Pope, & Keck, 1991). Similarly, worry and *rumination* show equally strong relations to anxiety and depression (Fresco, Frankel, Mennin, Turk, & Heimberg, 2002; McLaughlin et al., 2007). Watson and Kendall (1989, p. 498) noted that while depression should be associated with a focus on past loss and failures, research suggests "depressives tend to view the future pessimistically as an inevitable, hopeless extension of the past and present." Izard (2007, p. 267) similarly concluded that sadness, anger, and depression schemas co-vary "in many circumstances of daily life."

Research indicates that client improvement is associated with client verbalization of affect and affective processing (e.g., Diener, Hilsenroth, & Weinberger, 2007; Greenberg, Korman, & Paivio, 2001). Ultimately, the therapist aims to help the client process client affect to meet the client's therapeutic goals. Depending on the particular client and the therapist's theoretical orientation(s), this affective focus can help clients work through their problems, prepare for behavior change, or stop ruminating so that more adaptive cognitions (including meaning-making) can occur.

LISTEN FOR AFFECT IN STORIES

In personal narratives, emotional experience is the key marker of what is important (Greenberg & Angus, 2004). Consider what Robert Neimeyer (2001, p. xi), in the Preface to his book *Meaning Reconstruction and the Experience of Loss*, wrote about the personal impact of his father's suicide:

> When my father died on the eve of my 12th birthday, one world ended, and another began ... Our awareness of his suicide ... burst in on my sleeping 9-year-old brother and me the next morning in the form of our mother's panicked announcement that she could not wake our father. Frightened and bewildered, we scrambled out from under our cowboy quilt and stood peering around the doorjamb of our parent's bedroom, as our mother approached our father's lifeless body, touched him, and then recoiled in horror and a convulsion of tears. With that one abrupt gesture, most of what constituted the themes of our family narrative were swept away, and we were thrown collectively into a tumultuous renegotiation of who we were, how we would manage, and what his death meant. Many of the subsequent emotional, relational, and occupational choices made by my mother, my brother, my little sister, and me can be read as response to my father's fateful decision, although their meaning continues to be clarified, ambiguated, and reformulated across the years.

Neimeyer describes the feelings and experience of panic, fear, bewilderment, horror, and crying that marked his father's suicide, and influenced his and his family's subsequent choices about career and interpersonal relationships. As Habermas, Meier, and Mukhtar (2009, p. 752) documented, "negative experiences usually engender an increased effort to understand and deal with them."

From a narrative perspective, *always* listen for feelings: Emotions are the glue that holds the story together (Greenberg & Angus, 2004). Greenberg and Angus (2004) emphasize the importance of emotion in narrative work, suggesting that stories themselves are shaped by the emotional themes present. Since emotions function as signals of an individual's condition within a perceived environment (Campbell-Sills & Barlow, 2007), feelings inform individuals about their status in an actual or perceived environment. These signals function as powerful motivators for human activity.

> ***Client:*** I've spent years talking to everyone about how badly my husband treats me. I even tell him all the time to treat me better. None of it makes any difference.
>
> ***Therapist:*** You've been frustrated about the relationship for a long time.
>
> ***Client:*** It's like hitting my head against a wall. The same problems keep coming up again and again—he yells at me, he doesn't listen to me, he puts me down in front of our family. I get tired of it. A couple of times he even came close to hitting me.
>
> ***Therapist:*** You sound angry as you talk about Carlos.
>
> ***Client:*** Talking about it doesn't change Carlos. I think we should divorce.

The key feelings for this client are frustration and anger. In the example above, the emotion is associated with insight: The client realized that she talks to many people about her frustration with her spouse, but that talking about him does not change him; consequently, she decides to take action. The example above also illustrates a key therapy technique, empathic responses by the psychotherapist, for encouraging client recognition and expression of affect (Greenberg et al., 2001). Therapist behaviors such as reflection of feeling, restatement of content, and minimal encouragers can help focus clients on important affect-laden content (Egan, 2001).

Research suggests that clients' disclosures of emotionally charged narratives can lay the foundation for subsequent change in therapy (Greenberg & Angus, 2004). Clinicians help clients stay with and articulate their feelings, as this permits key narrative elements to emerge and constrains previous habitual interpretations. Retelling of a narrative provides "experiential access to those events" in the story (Hardtke & Angus, 2004, p. 252). The goal is for clients to differentiate those feelings and articulate "what was felt, in relation to whom, and about what issue ... leading to sustained elaboration of ... felt emotions" (Greenberg & Angus, 2004, pp. 338, 340). Similar to the Freudian concept of making the unconscious conscious, the client makes the previously wordless narrative scene explicit (Damasio, 1999).

PAY ATTENTION TO THE TIMING OF CLIENT EXPLORATIONS OF AFFECT

The timing of explorations about, expressions of, and experiencing feelings can be important. Clients during initial sessions commonly express strong feelings of distress; this may be particularly true for clients who have not sought therapy previously and who are seeking therapy voluntarily. Howard's research-supported phase model of psychotherapy (Howard, Moras, Brill, Martinovich, & Lutz, 1996) suggests that *remoralization* constitutes the first phase of psychotherapy (cf. Frankl, 2000). Therapists should listen for demoralization themes in initial sessions and provide a plausible rationale regarding hope for improvement. Many therapists do this by first normalizing the client's problems and then describing an approach to therapy that will alleviate the client's symptoms and presenting problems.

Therapists may not push for deeper feelings during initial session(s) because clients differ in their comfort and ability to express and explore moderate to intense feelings. More emotion is typically present in the beginning of storytelling and clients should not attempt to interpret their stories but allow them to flow out. Finding meaning in narratives occurs later in the process. Also, relationships with significant others are often a focal point of client stories, especially in the beginning of therapy. From a narrative perspective, this can become problematic when it prevents the exploration of the client's feelings. Consider an international student whose family has sent him to college with a particular vocational outcome in mind.

Client: My family wants me to become a doctor.

Therapist: What do you think about becoming a doctor?

Client: My father, uncle, and sister are doctors.

Therapist: So people in your family become doctors, and you're expected to do the same.

Client: Yes, my family is paying all of my tuition and expenses. My father wants to talk to you about my problems in school.

This information about the family tradition is certainly an important part of the client's story and likely an important reason for seeking therapy. But the psychotherapist will want to know the client's feelings.

Therapist: Okay, first tell me whether you want to become a doctor.

Client: I don't know.

Therapist: You're not sure...

Client: I really like my business classes better ... and I'm getting a C in Organic Chemistry! But there's no way my father will let me switch majors.

Some research on writing interventions suggests that self-referential activity early in the process is associated with successful outcomes (Pennebaker, Mehl, & Niederhoffer, 2003). That is, it is not the case that the client should totally ignore others' role in her or his problems, but that early on, the focus should be on the client's thoughts and feelings. Once clarified, discuss how the client should interact with others who are involved in a problematic situation.

Within a session, therapists frequently address feelings in the beginning and middle of sessions because discussions about affective content can generate considerable material. Leaving affect to be addressed in the last 5–10 minutes of a session can (a) lead to what feels like a forced ending (because the client often has more to say) and (b) inhibit therapeutic progress because the client lacks sufficient time to process and experience the feelings.

AS THE WORKING ALLIANCE DEVELOPS, EXPECT THE CLIENT'S STORY TO CHANGE AND DEEPEN

While most therapists see the development of a working alliance as an important first step in therapy, from a narrative perspective, the working alliance directly influences the content and quality of the stories the client shares with the therapist. Developing a working alliance is a prerequisite for many clients to be able to tell a deeper story about difficult-to-discuss feelings and issues. As a therapist in training observed about her work with a particular client, "it is important to develop a therapeutic alliance with the client before any of the 'work' can begin. Once this relationship was formed, my client was more open to discussing deeper issues and processing her emotions surrounding events" (C. Simonelli, personal communication, April 2010).

Telling a story to a skilled listener will help the formation of a working alliance (Hardtke & Angus, 2004). Anderson (2004) sees social bonds forming when therapist and client co-construct stories, while Boothe and Von Wyl (2004, p. 283) maintain that "listener and narrator are empathic partners in a narrative alliance."

Therapist: What's been going on?

Client: It's hard to talk about ... but I'm at the end of my rope.

Therapist: This is a really difficult time for you.

Client: Thanks. None of my friends understand what I'm going through.

Matching therapists' experiences, researchers have documented instances when individuals have initially been reluctant to fully disclose information related to their mental health (Bliese, Wright, Adler, Thomas, & Hoge, 2007; Meier & Schwartz, 2007; Milliken, Auchterlonie, & Hoge, 2007). Meier and Schwartz (2007), for example, found that some middle-school students tended to under-report socially undesirable problems at intake (e.g., cheating, smoking cigarettes). Developing the working alliance means that the client is more likely to self-disclose important information. When the working alliance does not develop relatively quickly, good therapists sense this lack of connection and the corresponding superficiality of the client's information.

In traditional approaches, diagnosis occurs at the beginning of therapy, typically on the basis of an intake interview. *Persistent relevance* (Beutler & Hamblin, 1986) refers to whether clients change their descriptions of core problems, over time, as therapy develops. If client themes change as the working alliance and rapport develop, therapists should be provisional in terms of their case conceptualizations, assessment tools for progress monitoring, and treatment planning. Theorists who write about case conceptualization observe that redefinition and clarification of client problems can occur throughout the therapy process (Battle et al., 1966; Hill, 1982; Madill, Widdicombe, & Barkham, 2001; Mash & Hunsley, 1993; Ridley, Li, & Hill, 1998).

IDENTIFY AND GROUND THE AFFECT IN NARRATIVES

Talking about feelings and thoughts can be difficult because they are fleeting, internal states. Skilled therapists identify and make clients' feelings and thoughts concrete by grounding them (Teyber & McClure, 2011), for example, in:

1. *Physical sensations* (asking the client to locate the feeling in a part of the body),
2. *Images* associated with the feeling (e.g., intense anxiety with the images remembered from an auto accident),

3. *Experiences* (e.g., feelings of shame in an adult, who remembers being repeatedly humiliated in particular social situations when he was an adolescent),
4. *Immediacy* (i.e., what the client is feeling at this moment),
5. *Physical objects* (e.g., such as an empty chair or physical places in the environment), and
6. *Summaries* (i.e., a listing or narrative of key elements).

Such grounding gives affect a psychological reality that can be employed as a reference point in future discussions of those feelings.

When experiencing feelings, clients may give nonverbal clues about how they physically feel when they are reporting affect (Meier & Davis, 2011, p. 25):

> ***Client:*** Even though it's been two years since Dad passed away, I still feel a hole in my life.
>
> ***Therapist:*** Tell me about that hole.
>
> ***Client:*** It's kind of an emptiness . . . a numbness.
>
> ***Therapist:*** You're holding your stomach as you talk about the emptiness. Hold your stomach a minute . . . tell me what you feel.
>
> ***Client:*** I feel . . . sad.

Gestalt therapists use clients' body movements, such as repeatedly making a fist or striking a pillow, to help strengthen clients' experience of feelings (Hardy, 1991; Perls, 1992). In the example above, the client might pay attention to his stomach to heighten awareness and experience feeling sad. Perls (1992) also employed an empty or two-chair technique, where a client would verbalize some component of their self and then switch to another chair to act out a different or contrasting part of the self. This is often a very effective way to help a client who has difficulty verbalizing material to tell multiple, conflicting stories or parts of stories.

With knowledge of the client's history, the therapist may be able to make it safer to share intense feelings by linking the current situation to a similar experience in the past:

> ***Client:*** Even though it's been two years since Dad passed away, I still feel a hole in my life.
>
> ***Therapist:*** Tell me about that hole.

Client: I can't . . . I don't know . . . (gently)

Therapist: Have you ever had this feeling before?

Client: Yes, when my grandmother died.

Therapist: Tell me about that, please.

Client: She helped raised me, took care of me for several years while my father was overseas serving in the Army.

Therapist: My sense is that it really hurt when she passed away.

Client: Very much.

Clients may also avoid experiencing in depth by talking rapidly or being verbose. One strategy is to interrupt nonstop talkers and *summarize* what you perceive as one or two key issues currently being discussed.

Client: Well, I certainly understand how my family and I get started on arguments. Everybody gets so involved in presenting their case that no one listens to the other. I know I get really frustrated in a hurry when no one listens to me. Last week we started to argue about my cell phone bill because my dad wants me to keep my texting below $50 a month. So I called my roommate and asked her how much she spent on cell phone texts a month . . . .

Therapist (interrupting): So you feel frustrated when no one listens to you.

Client: Right.

The therapist may also interrupt a verbose client by focusing on a key feeling. While the therapist in the example below may have allowed this client to talk for too long, the interruption—a focus on the client's evident anxiety—is effective in bringing the client's awareness to her affect. The example below is from counseling and therapy transcripts published by Alexander Street Press (2009) (www.alexanderstreet.com).

Patient: He called me and he's like, "What's wrong? You sound horrible." And I'm like, "I am. I really feel shitty today. I really feel lousy." And he's like, "Why?" And I was like, "It's just a lot of reasons." And he's like, "Because of me?" And I said, "Some of it." He said, "Do you want to break up?" I said, "No. Do you?" He said,

> "No." I said, "There's some things I need to talk to you about and I just am not happy anymore," I'm not happy with him. So he got really scared and he just . . . Some of the reasons I told him, you know, "You really have to start being more supportive and understanding of my feelings." I said, "I've been here for three years, and no matter what, even if I don't understand the way you feel, I'm still supportive of you, and you, you don't give that back to me and I need that back." And, you know, he understood that. And I talked to him about not really respecting my feelings, and he understood that too. But then later, like the next night when we had dinner, he—and I mean and he thought about it, for I didn't see him that night. And he called me and he's like, "I understand what you said and I love you and I—you know, you're right," and blah, blah, blah. Then the next night, when we talked about it more and I started to talk to him about my insecurities, and he's got this huge thing with people blaming him. He's like, "Not me, it's you." Because he thinks everybody's trying to blame him and point the finger at him, which I'm not. I'm just saying this is the way I feel and you have to understand it, you know, because he does. Because anybody who's going to deal with me has to understand the way I feel or accept the way I feel; they don't have a choice, just like I don't have a choice about anybody else's feelings. I can't control anybody else's feelings.

So we kind of—he got all mad, I don't know, and then he started saying all this stuff that I love you and I don't know why, you know . . . So that I'm just confused. I'm not sure where my feelings are coming from, if it's just my nature to feel that way and he triggers them, which some people will and some people won't, and that's okay, you know, and acceptable.

> ***Therapist:*** Can I stop you? Can I ask you how are you feeling now, you know? I mean, what's happening?
>
> ***Patient:*** Now I'm getting more anxious talking about it, yeah.

REPAIR AND EXTEND THE CLIENT'S EMOTION-RELATED STATEMENTS

Many clients lack the emotional vocabulary necessary to express what they feel beyond a basic dimension of positive or negative affect. As in the example below, they may employ generic labels like *upset* to describe what they feel.

Therapist: Last week you said that your father passed away two years ago, on this day.

Client: Yes ... I've been upset all week.

Therapist: As I listen to you talk, you seem ... sad.

Client: I don't understand what's wrong with me—it's been two years!

If you are the therapist for such a client, you may need to teach basic affective terms such as sad, angry, anxious, and fearful. This may be especially true when the client is a child, adolescent, or young adult (Hutchby, 2005). The therapist repairs or extends the client's affective description for the purpose of providing a more descriptive emotional label (Rae, 2008). This repair provides a psychological explanation for what the client is experiencing and opens the door for further exploration. In essence, the therapist is helping the client to create a deeper therapeutic story.

Therapist: Last week you said that your father passed away two years ago, on this day.

Client: Yes ... I've been upset all week.

Therapist: As I listen to you talk, you seem ... sad.

Client: I don't understand what's wrong with me—it's been two years!

Therapist: So you've been sad at times this week, the two-year anniversary of your father's passing.

Client: Yes, it surprises me because I have been feeling ok about it for months .... now it comes back ... I don't feel like I did when he first died, but I still miss him.

Therapist: So you haven't been feeling that sadness in a while, but the anniversary reminds you of that important loss, even though you weren't expected to feel this strongly about it.

Client: Yes ... I guess that makes sense.

In this example the therapist first substitutes the word "sad" for "upset," thus providing a more specific label for the client's affect. The client may or may not have agreed with this relabeling, but agrees and proceeds to provide more details. The therapist also suggests that the anniversary date of the father's passing unconsciously served as a reminder for the client to feel sad again. Also, the implication of this extension of the client's narrative about her "upset" feeling is that the feeling of sadness may return at future anniversaries or other dates and events associated with her father.

LISTEN FOR UNUSUAL AFFECTIVELY LADEN WORDS AND PHRASES

Clients will occasionally employ individual words and phrases that strike the listener as unusual or somehow out of place. The following dialog is from a well-known training video from the 1960s (Shostrom, 1965) used to demonstrate client-centered therapy. Carl Rogers is speaking with Gloria, a recently divorced mother who is expressing her ambivalence about her sexual desires (transcript edited from Wickman, 2000).

> ***Gloria:*** There's a girl at work who sort of mothers me .... I think she thinks I'm all sweet and I sure don't want to show my more ornery devilish side with her .... And it's so disappointing.
>
> ***Rogers:*** I get the disappointment, that here, a lot of these things you'd thought you'd worked through and now the guilts and the feeling that, only a part of you is acceptable to anybody else.
>
> ***Gloria:*** Regarding, for example, my sex life. This is the big thing. If I really fell in love with a man, and I respected him and I adored him, I don't think I'd feel so guilty going to bed with him and I don't think I'd have to make up any excuses to the children because they could see my natural caring for him.

While Gloria's description of her desires as a single woman are partially a result of the historical period in which this conversation occurred, "ornery devilish" is so strong a description that it indicates a significant conflict between her feelings about sex and her beliefs about appropriate behavior for a single woman in the 1960s. Wickman and Campbell (2003, p. 15) suggest that use of a term like "devil" indicates that Gloria's "existing frameworks for self-understanding and decision-making were no longer congruent with her new circumstance of being a recently divorced single mother." Clearly this would be useful material for further exploration. Similarly, Teyber and McClure (2011) used the term *compacted phrase* to describe a short phrase or sentence that clients employ repeatedly to communicate their emotional reaction to stressful events. Example phrases include "It's too much for me; I can't stand it" and "I've had it, I'm 'done,' I can't face any more" (Teyber & McClure, 2011, p. 201). That is, the client may have a relatively unique phrase that she or he employs repeatedly in therapy.

Students should also know that even experienced therapists can inadvertently employ unusual words in session, particularly when the client surprises them. The excerpt below is from a training videotape designed to provide examples of how therapists can handle a client's expression of sexual attraction toward the therapist (American Psychological Association, 1996). Here the client is expressing his interest in starting a romantic relationship with the female therapist because she listens so well to him:

> ***Client:*** Ever since my divorce, there's always something missing ... These women just don't understand me ... and that's what I really, really want and I really need ... I thought, well, you understand me.
>
> ***Therapist:*** So you were feeling like I could do better than those women in your life.
>
> ***Client:*** Yeah, you care about me. You show caring and love and ... these women ... that's what's missing from my life.
>
> ***Therapist:*** Well, I understand how delicious that can feel to be understood and cared about, which you are here .... It sounds like you might be suggesting you would like to have a romantic relationship with me.

In general, therapists try to avoid using unusual words with clients unless the client has introduced the word or phrase first. In the example above, students who watch this tape typically flag the word "delicious" as unusual because the client, while expressing attraction for the therapist, has used no language of this nature. In this example, the client may misinterpret the therapist's use of "delicious," perhaps as an indirect expression of romantic or sexual interest in the client—exactly the opposite result of what the therapist intended.

PAY ATTENTION TO AFFECTIVELY LADEN METAPHORS

A *metaphor* is "a figure of speech that contains an implied comparison—expressing an idea in terms of something else" (Meier & Davis, 2011, p. 29). Metaphors enable a therapist to provide a client with information about something that the person already understands, and then compare it to something that the person does not yet understand (Linehan, 1993).

Research suggests that people employ metaphors in everyday language quite often, as frequently as every 10–25 words (Geary, 2011). Lakoff and Johnson's (1980) work on conceptual metaphor indicates that metaphors take information from a source domain and place that information into a target domain. Typically, the source domain is a more concrete concept and the target domain a more abstract idea. Source domains include such basic topics as the body, animals, buildings, temperature, and food (Kovecses, 2002). As an example, Stott, Mansell, Salkovskis, Lavender, and Cartwright-Hatton (2010) described the metaphor of grasping: Since we can grasp physical objects—and most people easily understand this idea—we can use this basic concept to communicate when we say that we "grasp an idea." That is, in a sense we have somehow been able to understand an idea or put it within our control.

All psychotherapies and psychotherapists use metaphors, including Cognitive Therapy (Beck, 1979; Stott et al., 2010), psychodynamic psychotherapy (Arlow, 1979; Rasmussen & Angus, 1996), feminist therapy (Lee, 1997), multicultural therapy (Semmler & Braun, 2000), and Dialectical Behavior Therapy (Linehan, 1993). In cognitive therapy, for example, Beck noted that metaphors provide alternative ways of thinking for the client. Beck (1979) provided an example of a depressed client, experiencing suicidal thoughts, who early in therapy had said "I may feel like a mouse but I have the heart of a lion." Metaphors can be useful for communicating difficult or abstract meanings, for communicating with relatively few words, and for providing vivid information that can be more easily remembered (Stott et al., 2010). Metaphors have been used in psychotherapy to enable clients to communicate the qualities of their concerns and experiences, suggest solutions, help clients recognize conscious and (previously) unconscious aspects of self, reframe problems, change perspective on a topic by borrowing a term from another domain, combining topics to show something new, enhance flexibility, reorganize views of the self, and link thinking and feeling to allow for the representation of internal experience and expression of that experience in a coherent manner (Barker, 1985; Cirillo & Crider, 1995; Cummings, Hallberg, Slemon, & Martin, 1992; Kozak, 1992; Pistole, 2003).

Therapists may have favorite metaphors that they employ with clients to convey important messages. Stott et al. (2010) noted that with depressed clients who expect to recover quickly, the metaphor of a person with a broken leg can be employed to convey the message that improvement takes time, both with a broken leg and depression. From a therapist's perspective, one of the most important functions of metaphors is that they can convey abstract principles (Stott et al., 2010). Metaphors are a vehicle for therapists to convey sophisticated psychological concepts to clients, that is, to create new meaning for clients. Stott et al. (2010), for example, noted that for persons with posttraumatic stress disorder (PTSD), the notion of reexperiencing a traumatic memory might be compared to a duvet that is stuffed into a closet that is too small; the bedding continues to push the closet door open and fall out. Therapists have written books filled with examples of therapeutic metaphors of use to therapists and clients (e.g., Gordon, 1978). Kopp (1995) has also described methods for therapists to enable clients to explore and change the metaphors that clients present in therapy.

In ordinary conversations, when people employ metaphors we typically accept them at face value and assume that we have a general understanding of the content intended to be communicated. Therapists, however, will encourage clients to explore and elaborate on metaphors.

> ***Client:*** I guess I've let my world collapse. People at work have begun complaining about me. And I've been like a zombie most of the time.
>
> ***Therapist:*** Your world has collapsed?
>
> ***Client:*** I've been drinking again and missing a lot of work. My boss wants to know why I've missed the last two staff meetings.
>
> ***Therapist:*** Ok, you've been sober for two years. When did you start to drink again?
>
> ***Client:*** Management started to talk about layoffs when sales dropped last year. I was worried about what I would do if I got laid off—who would hire a 55-year-old man in this economy?
>
> ***Therapist:*** So you were anxious about losing your job.
>
> ***Client:*** Yes, and I was home sick one day, and I thought, what harm would one drink do? That was about two weeks ago, and between the stress and drinking, I've been a mess.

Phrases such as "let my world collapse" and "like a zombie" likely indicate strong affect (and possibly, its avoidance) associated with the events.

Clients may also present metaphors that can be usefully altered for therapeutic effect. Stott et al. (2010, p. 47) described the case of a client who described himself as "a bomb waiting to go off." This client had isolated himself from others in the hope that his pent-up anger might harm others, even though this had never actually happened. Exploration of the client's anger allowed the therapist to introduce a more benign metaphor of a pan of water boiling over and then simmering down. The therapist

TABLE 2.1 Examples of Metaphors Provided by Clients

"Yesterday I was talking with one of the drivers when my boss storms in and begins raking me over the coals for a work stoppage I had nothing to do with."
"I'm down in the dumps."
"These kids drive me up the wall."
"I learned yesterday that I've flunked out of school and that there's no recourse. I've seen everybody, but the door is shut tight."
"I guess I've let my world collapse. People at work have begun complaining about me. And I've been like a zombie most of the time."
"I feel like I am going to burst from loneliness."
"I feel as if I am a bomb waiting to go off."
"I put up this barrier against people so they don't really know me. It's like a brick wall."

Note: The list of client metaphors is drawn from Egan (2009), Hill (2004), and Stott et al. (2010).

and client could then begin to talk about methods for "turning the heat off" as one way to cope with the client's anger.

In practice, it is the unusual client who does not offer at least a few metaphors every session. Recognizing particular metaphors offered by an individual client can be helpful in terms of communicating with that person, conceptualizing client issues, and assessing client progress. Table 2.1 displays examples of client-provided metaphors.

CONSIDER THE AFFECTIVE IMPLICATIONS OF WHAT CLIENTS SAY

Every client story, from important incidents to client history, has potential *implications*. Implications refer to information provided by the client that indicates the presence of additional information that is not immediately obvious. Implications raise possibilities for exploring new knowledge and understandings based on the client's communications, both verbal and nonverbal.

Even the simplest statements and events have possible implications. For example, when I woke up in bed one morning, one of our family's cats walked on my chest and laid down, facing me. Possible implications include:

1. The cat likes me;
2. The cat was cold;

3. The cat thought I would pet it since the dog, who gets the most petting in our family, was asleep in the bed next to me;
4. The people who live in this house have too many animals.

The implications that therapists pay particular attention to in a therapy conversation are typically deeper or more affectively focused:

Therapist: You look frustrated and a bit angry right now as you talk about Carlos.

Client: It's like hitting my head against a wall. The same problems keep coming up again and again—he yells at me, he doesn't listen to me, he puts me down in front of our family . . . (*in a low voice*) I get tired of it.

Therapist: The way you said "I get tired of it" makes me think you feel . . . sad and disappointed, also?

Client: Yes. Carlos treated me so well for the first two years of our marriage and then . . .

The content of the client's statements, and the way she spoke, implied to the therapist a sense of loss and discouragement. The therapist tentatively shared her interpretation of the implications of the statement "I get tired of it" regarding a possible related feeling and the client confirmed that she also felt sad and disappointed. This opens new directions for exploration of the client's feelings and how those feelings developed in relation to the history of her relationship with her partner.

A therapist with good listening skills probes client statements for their affective implications. The therapist's ability to pick up on and discern implications in a client's story will depend upon a variety of factors, including the professional and personal experiences of the therapist as well as her or his knowledge of psychological and psychotherapeutic theories. Particularly with socially undesirable material that may be difficult for clients to report or discuss, therapists often consider the worst implications of what a client says.

Client: My father was a good dad, took good care of my mother and me and my little sister. He used to give me a lot of special attention.

Therapist: What kind of attention?

Client: Well ... sometimes he would come to my room in the middle of the night and get in bed with me.

Therapist: How old were you when this happened?

Client: I don't know ... he stopped when I was around 12.

Therapist: I guess when I hear about a man sleeping with a girl of that age, I think about the possibility of sexual abuse.

The client's description of this situation, in combination with the therapist's knowledge about the contexts of sexual abuse, led the therapist to inquire tentatively about the possibility of sexual abuse. Note that this client may or may not have been sexually abused. The therapist's recognition of that as a possible implication of her language, however, enabled further exploration of a potentially significant topic that the client may have been unwilling to bring up on her own.

As noted above, psychological theories are an important source of knowledge about therapy language and implications. Ellis suggested that Rational Emotive Behavior Therapists (REBT, 1998) pay attention to words like *must* and *should* as markers of irrational beliefs. Such concepts provide a framework for interpreting the meaning and possible implications of client's language.

Client: I *must* get an A on this test!

Therapist: Or ...?

Client: Without an A, I'm doomed!

The client in this example is obviously not literally doomed if she or he gets a grade of B or less. Instead, the words signal the personal significance of this test, perhaps for the grade in the course or for the student's overall grade point average and corresponding implications for getting into graduate school. As noted above, words like *must* and *should* are indicators of potential irrational beliefs in REBT (Ellis, 1998). While it is not the case that clients demonstrate an irrational belief every time they say *must* or *should* (e.g., "The weather forecast indicates it should rain tomorrow"), for the therapist with knowledge of REBT concepts such words are red flags that signal a potentially important direction for further exploration of the client's affect and cognitions. Knowing psychotherapy theories, consequently, means that therapists have a method for detecting and creating clinical implications on the basis of each client's language.

HELP CLIENTS LEARN TO PROCESS EMOTIONALLY LADEN CONTENT

With most clients, a major goal is for the therapist to help the client process the emotionally laden content of the client's narratives. Elliott and Greenberg (2001) listed several useful techniques, such as facilitating retelling of important events, two-chair dialog, and empty-chair work. Elliott and Greenberg (2001, p. 289) also provided several examples of what a therapist might say to facilitate emotional experiencing, including:

> ***Therapist:*** "Can you stay with that hurt and sadness for a minute, and just feel what that's about and what that's like?"
>
> ***Therapist:*** "One way to try to work with the grief is to put that part of you that you've lost in the chair and talk to her."

The key to this work centers on whether the client *experiences* the negative affect (NA) rather than just talks about or describes it. Clients must listen to feelings deeply before the emotionally laden material fades from attention.

With the empty-chair technique, clients appear to need to experience moderate to highly intense affect for the method to be successful (Hirscheimer, 1996, cited in Elliott & Greenberg, 2001). Research indicates that at least a moderate level of NA is required for positive change (Beutler & Harwood, 2000). Thus, with clients who present with little affect at the beginning of therapy, one of the first tasks is to help that individual get in touch with stronger NA. For many clients, experiencing NA can be considered a skill that requires practice and coaching. One client reported that he was aware of having a feeling, but could only stay with it for a second; we might consider this person at the beginning of practice for experiencing feelings.

Self-involving statements by the therapist are another method of helping clients who are inexperienced with experiencing affect or having difficulty being aware of NA. In contrast to *self-disclosure*, where the therapist talks about a personal feeling or experience, self-involving statements involve the therapist's reactions to some aspect of the client's experience (McCarthy, 1982; McCarthy & Betz, 1978; Watkins & Schneider, 1989). A client might have some difficulty, for example, getting in touch with feelings of sadness and grief around a complicated loss:

> ***Client:*** My father died about six months ago and I just don't feel anything.

Therapist: Okay, it would help me understand your feelings a bit better if you talked about your relationship with him.

Client: Well, when it became clear his illness was terminal over the past year or so, he began to turn the family business over to me. I haven't had much success starting a career in law and he thought this would solve two problems: I'd have a good job and someone would keep the business going.

Therapist: As you talk, I get a sense of some conflict in you.

Client: Yeah, I don't know.

Therapist: Even with your brief description about this complicated situation, I started to feel stressed.

Client: You did?

Therapist: Yes. I can imagine you might have been feeling sad and anxious about your dad's illness and impending passing .... You might also be feeling conflicted about giving up your law career and ... wondering if you have the management skills to run what was *his* business.

Client: Yeah ... but I was also happy by the idea of finally having a job where I could make a living. But I don't know.

Therapist: That's a lot of different feelings to sort out, positive and negative. I can understand how it might feel overwhelming at times.

Client: Definitely.

Therapist: Well, this is a good place to begin to sort these feelings.

Client: Okay.

In this example the therapist's self-involving statement about feeling stressed by the client's complicated life situation resonated with the client. It may have normalized the feelings for the client and made it okay to begin to share the different, conflicting feelings he had and was experiencing only briefly. In addition, the therapist is modeling how to experience and express NA.

Research summaries indicate that depth of client experiencing in therapy is associated with positive client change (Greenberg et al., 2001).

Goldman (1997, cited in Greenberg et al., 2001), for example, found that clients with positive outcomes show an increase across sessions on depth of processing on core issues. Interestingly, increase in depth of processing better predicted outcome than working alliance (Goldman, 1997). As clients deepen and broaden their exploration of emotionally laden content, they begin to make sense of and resolve their problematic situation(s). In the edited dialog below, Greenberg et al. (2001) describe an adult client in her mid-40s who continues to struggle with the fact that her mother kicked her out of the house when she was a teenager and pregnant. The therapist is asking what the client would say to her mother (still living) if she were present in the therapy session:

Therapist: Say something to her.

Client: (Sobbing) I can't, I can't believe what you did to me. (Sighs) I can't believe that you did that to me. That you put me in that situation. That was worse than, than death.

Therapist: Tell her, "I'm angry at you."

Client: I'm angry at you for that. How could you just behave so despicably?

Therapist: That's good. Say some more to her.

Client: I was just a . . . sad, lonely 16-year-old, and where was my mother? Nowhere. You didn't come. You didn't care. You just left me.

Therapist: What could she have done to show that she cared?

Client: You could have just, just thrown that pride of yours by the wayside and come, driving up to where I lived and bursting in to see what was going on with your own daughter . . . . And then to care, you know, to sort of help me along through this, and relieve me of some of the difficulty of it.

Therapist: What are you feeling now?

Client: (Crying). I just feel so sad for me as a young mother. I was so alone and so needed someone to love me. But I was not bad, unworthy. Actually I was very courageous, my mother just couldn't cope.

Greenberg et al. (2001) reported that therapy helped this woman deal with her unfinished business with her mother. Her depth of experiencing helped to create new meaning for the situation, that her mother was mistaken and that she (the client) was not a bad person. When therapy ended, the client's symptoms had decreased and she was able to form a more caring relationship with her mother. She had also reevaluated her self-description of how she performed as a young mother.

SUMMARY AND IMPLICATIONS

The principles and guidelines described in this chapter encourage therapists to focus on affect in client narratives and to help clients experience and process their feelings about problematic situations. The narrative perspective emphasizes that it is the therapist who helps the client explore narratives in a therapeutic manner—therapy is not an ordinary conversation about difficult events. Particularly around topics with NA, the therapeutic process helps the client to select, identify, name, communicate, elaborate on, and deepen the client's emotional experience. Because of the difficulties most people experience when faced with intense NA, the chapter also notes some of the potential obstacles in the therapeutic process, a topic more fully described in Chapter 5.

For most people, telling their feelings and experiences to another person validates those feelings and experiences. When another person has heard you, the feelings and experiences become *real*. Thus, to perform most of the behaviors described in this chapter, therapists require good listening skills (Meier & Davis, 2011). Skilled listeners help the client attend to and express what she or he is experiencing at this moment, particularly NA and associated content. A client's ability to tell her or his stories depends upon a number of factors, including the relationship that develops with a particular therapist as well as the client's comfort and experience with expressing emotions, often about socially difficult experiences. But the person who experiences or produces a fuller description of him- or herself has changed that self-description in an important way. As Anderson (2004, p. 327) summarized:

> Our stories offer the opportunity for a uniquely creative human activity or a flow of concentration and experiencing (Csikszentmihaly, 1993). In such moments, stories transcend the simple concatenation of events, and the participants attempt to reexperience the event by becoming totally engrossed in the retelling of those interpersonal interactions, experiencing the events as if they were happening anew. A picture may paint a thousand words, but a good narrator can breathe life into the same portrait

a thousand times and even tell a different story each time, a new experience with each listener.

This exploration and elaboration work is another way of describing a *corrective emotional experience* (Teyber & McClure, 2011) in which clients reenact and reexperience events in their stories (Anderson, 2004). Greenberg and Angus (2004, p. 333) report that their preliminary results with single cases indicate that "clients' disclosures of emotionally charged personal narratives is foundational to the process of change." When strong feelings are not addressed, however, therapy "stalls and loses meaning" (Teyber & McClure, 2011, p. 186).

Timing matters. Discussing his mother's impending death, Neimeyer (2001, p. xii) wrote that "the immediacy of this real and impending loss makes any very specific anticipation of its meaning impossible." The focus during and in anticipation of a crisis or another emotionally intense event should be affect; turning the client's attention toward resolution and meaning-making occurs once the affective exploration has been sufficient and thorough for the particular client. The clinical and research literature also indicate that a cathartic approach may by itself be inadequate. Samoilov and Goldfried (1998, p. 380) cited Foa and Jaycox's (1999) model of chronic PTSD, which indicates that such individuals "tend to see the world as extremely threatening and themselves as very fragile, unable to handle stress." After clients process emotional material, the therapist and client can discuss alternative meanings for the problematic events and situations that trouble the client. This cognitive, meaning-making process, what facilitates and impedes it, is the focus of the next chapter.

Three

Cognitive Elements of Narratives

Events that cause psychological distress in individuals usually lead to cognitive efforts to solve or resolve those problems. Neimeyer (2001, p. xxi) observed that "loss, and our personal, relational, and cultural responses to it . . . initiates a quest for meaning in deeply personal and intricately social terms." Listening to clients' emotional concerns and validating them is a corrective emotional experience (Teyber & McClure, 2011), and helping clients to find meaning in their feelings and experiences, to make sense of them, is a viable path to therapeutic change. The principles in Chapter 3 describe what therapists can say and do to facilitate clients' efforts with *meaning-making* and related cognitive interventions in the therapeutic process.

From a narrative perspective, each individual speaks a language that is both shared by others and relatively unique to that person. Communication between therapist and client becomes more complicated to the extent that they differ on variables such as native language, culture, ethnicity, gender, religion, socioeconomic status, sexual orientation, occupation, and age. In terms of cultural competence, the therapist should be sensitive when the client is a non-native speaker of the client's language. Given that the nuances of verbal and nonverbal communication may be different across cultures, therapists should be careful to check out the meaning of client statements and stories. It may also be important to be certain that the client understands the meaning of the therapist's statements; this may require the therapist to be more active and explanatory than normal.

ACCEPT NARRATIVES IN WHATEVER FORM THEY ARE OFFERED

Particularly in the beginning, therapists are wise to accept client narratives in whatever form they are offered. For many clients, *self-report* of embarrassing or shaming problems is simply too difficult until they have developed a stronger working alliance. Therapists' theoretical orientation, however, may make it difficult to accept certain types of information from clients. A behavior therapist who does not believe in the validity of dream interpretation, for example, may be reluctant to spend therapy time exploring the dreams of clients who want to report and discuss them in therapy. Viney (1993) discussed the case of June:

> ***Therapist:*** Well, you tell me about the dream.
>
> ***June:*** Oh well, the first one was, um, there was a lady there. And she said, "You've done so and so." I just forget who it was. It wasn't terribly important what she'd accused me of; but I suppose it bugs me. The next thing, her husband stood behind her and said, "No, June didn't do that."
>
> ***Therapist:*** Do you have any ideas about what the dream means to you?
>
> ***June:*** Well, the first thing is false accusation, you know. I don't know where people dream up these things, you know. It's my dream, but why people think I'm guilty of such and such, you know.

Clients who report dreams without prompting by the therapist may be individuals who have difficulty directly accessing difficult material or expressing their feelings about such content. Dreams may offer these individuals safe psychological distance when discussing threatening personal issues.

Although uncommon, clients can provide personal accounts through a variety of forms beyond conversation with the therapist. More artistically inclined clients, for example, may come into a session with a journal, drawings, or photographs. Emails or phone messages are other ways clients may provide clinically relevant stories. Children in play therapy may be able to tell stories about characters in games that provide insights into psychological states and difficulties. The key for therapists is to be open and flexible about listening to these narratives.

The form in which the narrative is delivered may also be diagnostic of the client's rate of progress in therapy. A client who reports affectively laden dreams, for example, but has difficulty expressing her feelings in session, is likely to need more time to work through affect than an individual who can directly discuss emotions. The process of talking about dreams in therapy also provides the client with an opportunity to learn how to directly express affect through language as compared to more indirect (but psychologically safer) methods like dreams.

LISTEN FOR RECURRENT THEMES, AND EXCEPTIONS

Many clients repeat stories, doing what Madigan (2011, p. 33) described as "saturated tellings of these problems stories." As described in Chapter 2, *persistent relevance* refers to whether initial client problems remain the focus of client attention or whether different problems appear as therapy progresses (Beutler & Hamblin, 1986). In general, the therapist should listen for recurrent themes. Client stories are typically organized around themes, which "link events of their lives in sequences through time" (Madigan, 2011, p. 34). Clients' recurrent themes are likely to possess strong emotional components; Linehan (1993, p. 44) summarized research that noted that "increases in emotional arousal and intensity narrow attention, so that emotion-relevant stimuli become more salient and are more closely attended to." It would be unusual, and worthy of further attention by the therapist, if a client repeatedly discussed a theme without expressing some type of emotion related to that theme. Such a condition implies that the individual is inhibiting or interfering with the activation of relevant emotion (Linehan, 1993). This *avoidance* is likely to result in rumination, with thoughts and feelings breaching into awareness, often at times when the person is not actively engaged in their environment (e.g., breaks at work or school, taking a shower before sleeping).

Table 3.1 contains one therapist-in-training's description of client themes during the first five sessions. Graduate students whose training includes audio- or videotaping sessions have the advantage of being able to listen repeatedly to or view sessions to record themes and other observations. Over those sessions the therapist decided that she could identify 15 themes from progress notes with this client, an international graduate student in a U.S. university. Most themes are present only once or twice across sessions, but *funding concerns* and *stress over thesis* were present for multiple sessions. Two initial concerns, *anxiety and stress* and *frustration,* are likely present in subsequent sessions (as accompaniments to other problems) but may not have been named themes or issues by the client or therapist beyond Session 1. This table is discussed in more detail in Chapter 6, "Assessment."

One of the issues with identifying current themes is that different therapists are likely to hear, and perhaps elicit, different themes with the same (hypothetical) client. That is, any client is likely to report different issues with different therapists (cf. Gloria's different presentation with Rogers, Perls, and Ellis in Shostrum, 1966). Research on *case conceptualization* and diagnostic interviewing also suggests that clinicians are likely to identify different issues with the same client (Meier, 2003). So, supervision and consultation with colleagues may be particularly important with failing clients so that previously unnoticed themes may be eventually identified.

TABLE 3.1 Continuing and Changing Themes During the First Five Sessions of an International Graduate Student Client

	Session				
Theme	1	2	3	4	5
Anxiety and stress	X				
Frustration	X				
Stay here vs. Argentina	X				X
Funding concerns	X	X	X	X	
Lack of motivation	X			X	
Racist comments		X			
Social life		X		X	
Interpersonal conflict		X	X		
Stress over thesis		X	X		X
Perfectionism			X		
No balance			X		
Romantic relationship				X	
Lack of academic support			X		X
School ending					X
More productive weekend					X

In addition to noticing recurrent themes, for most clients it is also important to note reports of information that conflict with the client's dominant themes and narratives. Polkinghorne (2004) described *deconstruction* as the process of helping clients to identify and take apart the domain plot in their lives. The client becomes aware of the dominant story and questions its elements so that this narrative becomes just one possible view of the self. Given that most client stories fail to include all relevant experiences and feelings (Bruner, 1990), therapists can probe and help clients identify what narrative therapists call *unique outcomes* (Madigan, 2011). These are the neglected or forgotten aspects of clients' lives, the exceptions to the story themes. Unique outcomes provide a method of talking "outside the restraints of the problem-saturated story being told" (Madigan, 2011, p. 34). Over the course of therapy the therapist can help the client to elaborate and deepen—to thicken, in qualitative research language—these forgotten or neglected aspects, thus allowing the reauthoring of new narratives.

Linehan (1993, p. 218) presented a similar conception regarding assessment in Dialectical Behavior Therapy (DBT):

> Dialectical assessment requires that the therapist, along with the patient, constantly look for what is missing from individual or personal explanations of current behaviors and events. The question always being asked is "What is being left out here?" The assessment does not stop at the immediate environment, or at the historical family or other past learning experiences (although these are not ignored); it also examines social, political, and economic influences on the patient's current behavior.

Madigan (2011) noted that revised narratives can include new proposals for action and describe the circumstances likely to support these new action proposals. Other life events become incorporated more fully into the story and the client is placed as a more active protagonist; essentially, the narrative expands and becomes more flexible.

A person who has experienced trauma and abuse by another person, for example, may be constrained by the other's narrative of what occurred (Madigan, 2011). A child who was sexually abused by her father, for example, may have been told that she enjoyed the sexual experience and continues to believe that account. Similarly, narratives that locate the problem entirely within the person may be reauthored by taking contexts into consideration. In social contexts, important influences include gender and race (Lee, 1997), and narrative therapists will help clients deconstruct dominant cultural themes such as inferiority and superiority (Semmler & Braun, 2000).

Semmler and Braun (2000) discussed the case of Shirley, an African American graduate student who was the first member of her family to pursue a graduate degree. She came to therapy complaining about feelings of depression and lacking confidence in her ability to complete her degree; her family appeared to have little understanding of her academic activities. Attending a predominantly White university in a White community, Shirley wondered whether her professors and fellow students doubted her intellectual abilities. Semmler and Braun (2000) noted that a narrative therapy approach with Shirley involved asking her questions such as: How were you recruited into thinking of yourself as inferior? What was the training ground for your feelings of inferiority? Shirley recalled racist incidents in her life, including a high-school counselor who questioned whether she could handle college work despite high grades and test scores. She also recalled that her family had instilled in her a work ethic that maintained that hard work could overcome any social barrier, including racism. Although Shirley sometimes forgot this competent sense of self, Semmler and Braun (2000) maintained that when she recalled this self-description it helped her reauthor the dominant culture's description of African Americans as academically inferior.

NOTICE ILL-FORMED, INCOMPLETE, AND DISTORTED DESCRIPTIONS

A basic premise of narrative approaches is that *how* people describe themselves, their environments, and their lives provides important information about personal problems. One way to assess those descriptions is to consider instances when individuals' statements are perceived as *ill-formed* or *incomplete* (Bandler & Grinder, 1975). This can be true at different levels of language: Specific words, phrases and sentences, paragraphs, and whole stories can be vague in their meanings. Several approaches to therapy have the concept of maladaptive themes as central to their approach (e.g., schema therapy; Young, Klosko, & Weishaar, 2003).

From a linguistic perspective, distorted statements can be characterized in terms of biases such as *generalizations* and *deletions* (Bandler & Grinder, 1975). Generalizations are ideas about the world or how we operate in it that are not literally true. With deletions we selectively focus on certain aspects of our environment and ignore other components. Therapists who pay attention to client language listen for, explore, and eventually try to deepen these distortions.

> ***Client:*** People scare me. I get scared when I'm away from home.
>
> ***Therapist:*** All people?
>
> ***Client:*** No . . . mostly just other kids at school, other guys.
>
> ***Therapist:*** So all guys at your high school scare you.
>
> ***Client:*** The kids who hit me or say they're going to hit me.
>
> ***Therapist:*** So you're not afraid of the teachers, girls, or even most of the guys—it's the bullies who scare you.
>
> ***Client:*** Yeah!

These ideas fit well with Beck's (1979) Cognitive Therapy concepts about dysfunctional thinking and associated emotional responses. Beck's approach focuses on such cognitive errors as all-or-nothing thinking and overgeneralizations. In general, psychological and psychotherapy theories provide a strong basis for evaluating client stories. The stronger the therapist's knowledge of diverse theoretical orientations, the deeper and more elaborate the filters the therapist can apply to consider what is missing or distorted in client expressions.

Therapists' reactions to client narratives can also signal a need for further exploration of potential distortions. A therapist working in an inpatient hospital, for example, related how one of his patients came into therapy with a letter from his sister. The patient described the letter as highly critical of the patient and very manipulative in its portrayal of events in the family, and offered the letter to the therapist as proof of his beliefs of having been wronged by his family. The therapist was quite puzzled, even offended, when he began to read the letter, which appeared to be quite understanding and supportive of the patient, even of his serious misbehaviors. From a narrative perspective, two key questions to consider here are: What assumptions and history does the patient have with his family and sister that would lead him to substantially distort this communication? What motivation would the patient have to distort this communication? In other words, assume that the patient's depiction makes sense *in some way* that is not readily apparent to others. In what way might the therapist make sense of the patient's story about his interactions with his family?

While many psychotherapy theories place the source of distorted cognitions within the client, the groups, institutions, and cultures in which the client lives can also be a source of incomplete self-descriptions. Madigan (2011, pp. 23–25) provided a dialog with an individual, Tom (and his wife, Jane), whose self-descriptions appear distorted by his time as an inpatient being treated for depression:

> ***Therapist:*** Tom, do you think this bored and unaccomplished sense of yourself is a final description of yourself?
>
> ***Client:*** Maybe not.
>
> ***Therapist:*** Tom, why do you think this bored and unaccomplished sense of yourself might not be a final description of yourself?
>
> ***Client:*** It might be the shock treatment, because it makes me slow and I can't remember much. I retired and didn't know what to do and I feel like a rock on the end of a piece of rope.
>
> ***Therapist:*** What does feeling like a rock on the end of a rope feel like?
>
> ***Client:*** Lousy, like I have nowhere to turn—just hanging here.

Therapist: Is there someplace you would rather be?

Client: As the bumper sticker on my car says—I'd rather be gardening.

Therapist: And what would you grow?

Client: I'm not sure the hospital would let me grow anything.

Therapist: Tom, if you get back to growing up things in your life, what would you grow?

Client: I'd like to grow heirloom tomatoes again and see all their weird colors and shapes and maybe watch my grandkids grow.

Therapist: If you were able to take this step to grow a bit of yourself back, what do you believe you might be stepping toward?

Client: I'd get myself out of the madhouse!

Therapist: Is there one particular aspect of yourself that most wants and supports you to move out of the madhouse?

Client: The part of me that wants to be free.

Therapist: Can you remember a time in your recent or distant past when you felt that you were free?

Client: Yes, many times, like when I was gardening and when I was playing hockey with my old friends on Tuesday nights, or even just shoveling the snow off the driveway.

Therapist: Tom, is the hospital's description of you as a chronically depressed person an accurate description of you?

Client: No, I think they helped me get worse.

Therapist: In what ways do you feel that the hospital has made you feel worse about yourself?

Client: Well, being with them a year or so I haven't gotten any better, and I think that they are giving up—this is why they sent me to you [laughs]—you're the last stop and they weren't much help anyway. Most of them are nice, but you know.

While Madigan (2011) presented the above dialog as an example of narrative therapy, it can also be seen as an initial step in *problem solving*. Heppner, Cooper, Mulholland, and Wei (2001, p. 330) noted that problem solving has been "repeatedly conceptualized as central to psychotherapy for decades." Problem-solving approaches focus on elements such as client perception of the problems—which the therapist above emphasized with Tom—as well as strategies to alleviate the problem.

TEST THE NARRATIVE

People can sometimes confuse their thoughts and feelings with actual events and consequences in the environment (Linehan, 1993). A student, for example, who anxiously thinks "I must get an A on this test" is acting as if a poor outcome on the exam might be physical harm. Barlow et al. (2011) similarly wrote that cognitive misappraisals are associated with the experience of strong negative affect such as anxiety. Two such misappraisals are *probability overestimation*, where the likelihood of a feared event is exaggerated in client accounts, and *catastrophizing*, where the negative consequences are exaggerated and one's ability to handle those consequences are underestimated (Barlow et al., 2011). Barlow et al. (2011) suggests that such misappraisals become problematic when they are automatically applied, independent of the actual environment.

In general, cognitive therapists ask clients who suffer from such irrational descriptions to provide evidence for these thoughts. To counter probability overestimation, for example, a therapist might work through the probability of a feared event actually occurring, based on general information and the client's personal experience. Consider a client who has developed a fear of flying after a friend died in a plane crash:

> ***Therapist:*** So you developed your fear of flying after your friend died on the plane that crashed near here.
>
> ***Client:*** Yes . . . she was on a short commuter flight.
>
> ***Therapist:*** So you cannot fly at all, even though you need to fly because of business and family visits?
>
> ***Client:*** No, I feel ok to travel on long flights. I travel regularly from the US to Europe and back, and the long flights don't bother me. I can't take short flights.
>
> ***Therapist:*** So it is the length of the flight that scares you.

Client: Yes. If the flight is longer than an hour, I feel comfortable.

Therapist: What is it about shorter flights that is terrifying?

Client: I don't know.

Therapist: Because it happened here, I recall that your friend was flying a commuter airline that uses propeller airplanes. And they were flying in poor weather conditions.

Client: I didn't know that.

Information may be helpful for some clients; for others like the client above, loss of control may be more salient. Therapists may wish to explore the irrationality of a risk-free life and that vulnerability and loss of control are a natural part of life.

NOTICE THE CLIENT'S SELF-DESCRIPTIONS ABOUT PERSONAL AGENCY

One of the most theoretically interesting and empirically supported approaches to self-descriptions is Bandura's self-efficacy theory (Bandura, 1977, 1997). As shown in Figure 3.1 (adapted from Bandura, 1977), *self-efficacy* refers to an individual's expectations about whether she or he can perform the behavior(s) necessary to produce desired outcomes. A graduate student facing a comprehensive examination, for example, may know that if he or she studies for three months of intense study, this will result in passing the examination; these are *outcome expectations* about what behaviors will produce desired outcomes. The student's expectations about whether she can study for that length of time, however, are likely to influence her initiation and persistence of study behaviors (Bandura, 1977, 1986, 1997). Students with low self-efficacy for studying are likely to feel

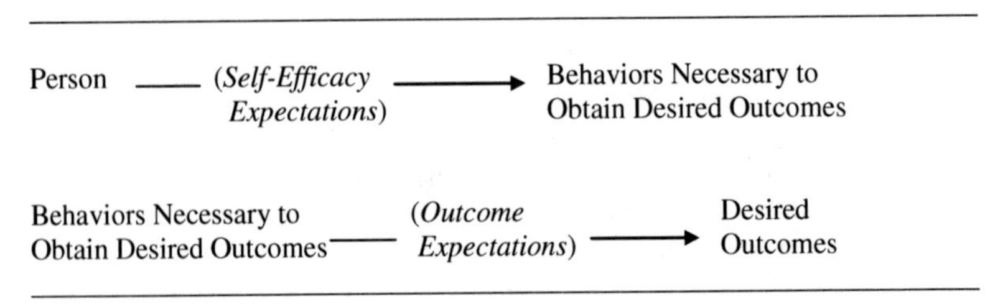

FIGURE 3.1 *Expectations for efficacy and outcomes.*

anxious about making such efforts. Research on self-efficacy expectations have generally supported Bandura's theory and have included studies examining self-efficacy in a variety of domains, including mental health, athletic performance, and career choice (e.g., Bandura, 1977, 1997).

Theoretically, self-efficacy can be applied to most client problems. What follows is a self-efficacy analysis of a client–therapist dialog, edited and shortened from a YouTube video (http://www.youtube.com/watch?v=7O45nSwxDJ8&feature=fvw) of a role-play between two graduate students. The client is a social phobic in his first session with a client-centered counselor.

> ***Client:*** I guess I've been having problems.
>
> ***Therapist:*** There are some things you've been struggling with?
>
> ***Client:*** Yeah, it's ... I don't know. I've tried talking about this to someone before, but I ... I just couldn't.
>
> ***Therapist:*** It seems like you feel overwhelmed when you think about these things that you've been struggling with. Like, I know there's something wrong but I can't quite put it into words. Is that right?
>
> ***Client:*** Yeah, I ... I just don't know. I don't really like to think about it, so that's part of the reason why I didn't want to come here today, but my roommate insisted.
>
> ***Therapist:*** It's really difficult talking about these things.
>
> ***Client:*** Yeah.

Words like "can" or "couldn't" communicate the individual's expectations for performing relevant behaviors. From this initial interchange it appears that the client wants to talk about his personal problems, and sees benefits for doing so, but has low self-efficacy for talking about problems ("I've tried talking to someone about this before, but I ... I just couldn't"). Two implications of this difficulty are that the client may also experience difficulties talking with other people in general (e.g., initiating conversations with strangers) as well as talking about himself to other people (e.g., even to friends who might provide social support).

Therapists should also listen in client narratives for the sources of the evaluative component of self-descriptions. One of the key elements for many clients in gauging the severity of their mental health issues is social comparison. That is, compared to friends and family, how severe are the problem(s) that have brought the client into therapy? Family and friends may also explicitly provide information about the need for psychotherapy, as did the client's roommate in the example above. Another major source is culture, which provides a repertoire of life stories that can be adopted by persons living in that culture (Polkinghorne, 2004). In a therapy context, some cultural stories can be "constrictive and blaming" (Polkinghorne, 2004, p. 53), and narrative therapists then see their therapeutic task as helping clients to create more expansive interpretations of clients' situations. In many Western societies, for example, the majority culture presents thin women as attractive and desirable, contributing to the development of eating disorders (Zinn, 2006). To counter these influences, Madigan (2011) described the development of an Anti-Anorexia/Bulimia League. Epston (2009) created *leagues* of individuals who have experienced and developed knowledge of various problems, including bullying and eating disorders, and began to accumulate their knowledge in archives. Madigan's (2011) league includes a group of women and therapists who meet regularly to provide public education and political activism around eating disorders, including cultural practices of objectification of women.

HELP CLIENTS RESOLVE POLARITIES TO CREATE NEW MEANINGS

Kelly (1955) maintained that cognitive constructs contain opposite poles or ends of a continuum; in other words, constructs typically can be described in terms of similarities and opposites. Constructs are based on an individual's experience of the world and also influence what the individual expects to experience in the future. Individuals in psychological distress often appear to be stuck on one end of the continuum, or flip between the opposing poles, when they talk about problem-related constructs.

This phenomenon is apparent with many clients in distress, but most obvious with persons classified as Borderline Personality Disorder (BPD, American Psychiatric Association, 2000). DBT was initially developed for therapeutic work with individuals diagnosed as BPD; Linehan (1993, p. 35) describes DBT as "engaging a person in dialogue so that movement can be made." DBT emphasizes *dialectics* which Linehan (1993) describes as "the reconciliation of opposites in a continual process of synthesis" (p. 19), helping clients "change by persuasion and by making use of the oppositions inherent in the therapeutic relationship" (p. 34). Linehan (1993, p. 35) further describes the therapy process as "through the therapeutic opposition of contradictory positions, both patient and therapist can arrive at new meanings within old meanings."

Therapists often view borderline clients as particularly difficult to treat. Linehan (1993) maintained that borderline and suicidal individuals vacillate between contradictory positions or beliefs ("I am bad" versus "I am good"). Known as *splitting*, borderlines can become stuck in one or the other position when describing themselves or others. Linehan (1993, p. 35) described such a conflict as a "dialectical failure" when one is unable to resolve the contradictory positions. The dialectic approach can be applied both to the client's conceptualizations of problems and the therapeutic relationship and process. The therapist aims to balance acceptance and change, flexibility and stability, nurturing and challenge, limitations and opportunities—and models and teaches this approach to clients. The DBT therapist, for example, combines acceptance and change strategies: Accept the client as to who they are currently, and look for opportunities to change. Linehan (1993, p. 201) wrote that "No rigid position is possible, and process and change are inevitable."

The main strategy of motivational interviewing (Arkowitz, Westra, Miller, & Rollnick, 2008) can be conceptualized as helping the client move between the polarities of pros and cons about change. Barlow et al. (2011, pp. 44–45) presented the following (edited) dialog of a client with panic attacks discussing the polarities of behavior change:

> ***Therapist:*** Ok, now let's look at some of the pros for staying the same. What did you come up with?
>
> ***Client:*** I don't really think there are any benefits to staying the same.
>
> ***Therapist:*** What do you think has held you back from changing this before you came into treatment?
>
> ***Client:*** Well, changing on my own was just so much work.
>
> ***Therapist:*** It sounds like one of your pros for staying the same might be that it is simply easier to stay the same. Now, what are some of the cons for staying the same?
>
> ***Client:*** Well, the ways things are kind of stinks. I mean, I can't do a lot of the things I want to be able to do, like travel or go out with friends.
>
> ***Therapist:*** You mentioned that one of the benefits for staying the same was that it was easier. How much work is it for you to try and manage your panic now?
>
> ***Client:*** It's a lot of work. In fact, it's pretty exhausting to constantly be on guard for situations that are going to make me panic.

CHANGE MEANING BY SHIFTING THE CLIENT'S PERCEIVED CONTEXT

Psychophysical research, focused on investigating phenomena such as sensory detection and pain thresholds, typically is not a source of information seen as relevant to counseling and psychotherapy. More recent findings, however, fit well with and inform mental health professionals interested in narratives and language. Perhaps the most relevant finding is that to perceive the characteristics of any object, individuals must notice context and change over time in the object (Lockhead, 1992, 1995). The apparent size of an object, for example, depends on the context in which it is seen; change the context, and the apparent size of the object also changes. Discussing the work of Gregory Bateson, White and Epston (1990, p. 2) reported that Bateson maintained that "all information is necessarily 'news of difference,' and that it is the perception of difference that triggers all new responses in living systems." Similarly, Bateson "demonstrated how the mapping of events through *time* is essential for the perception of difference, for the detection of change" (White & Epston, 1990, p. 2).

Thus, a critical narrative task for therapists is to recognize and understand client contexts in narratives. One of the difficulties in understanding client contexts and worldviews is that they may be so implicit that the client has forgotten them. But because people in general endeavor to communicate in a way that contributes to the goals of the conversation (Grice, 1991; Schwarz, 2010), any statement in a conversation should be assumed to be relevant to the aim of the conversation and thus may provide information about the contexts.

Consider a multicultural client who has moved to the United States in the past year and presents with persistent sadness and depression that she does not understand. In Spain she had a position as manager of a bank, but her husband accepted a long-term job transfer to the United States and insisted on moving the family, including their three young children. Within six months of moving, the client's father died unexpectedly, and she returned to Spain for six weeks to help her mother cope with the loss.

Client: I feel so sad, so depressed.

Therapist: You've lost a lot in the past year.

Client: Yes . . .

Therapist: You moved to a new city, leaving your job and friends behind.

> ***Client:*** Yes, and I can't find a new job here that's as good as the one I had.
>
> ***Therapist:*** Your father passed away this fall and you went back to Spain to take care of your mother.
>
> ***Client:*** Sometimes I will just start crying, for no reason.
>
> ***Therapist:*** You've had major changes in your life, in a relatively short period of time.
>
> ***Client:*** I know. (crying softly)
>
> ***Therapist:*** But you've done all of this for a reason, a very good reason. You left your job and friends to accompany your husband to his new job, to be with your children. And even though it was more comfortable for you to be in Spain than here, you came back to take care of your children, to support your husband and family.
>
> ***Client:*** That's true. I want to be a good mom and wife.
>
> ***Therapist:*** You've sacrificed to be a good mom.
>
> ***Client:*** Yes, that's why.

So the therapist helped the client to remember that her current losses and sadness were part of significant sacrifices she made to be with and take care of her children and husband. In this conversation, the context for the client changed: The client was not simply sad and alone in a new city, but she was sad because of sacrifices she made for what she had previously described as a major purpose in her life, to be a good mother and wife. Although her sadness would decrease as she made new friends and started working again, the feeling made sense to her as a reminder of her choices and priorities.

While most therapies place problems within the client, *externalizing the problem* provides an opportunity for client and therapist to think differently by changing the context of the *problem's location*. Madigan (2011, p. 18) summarized White's approach:

> White's therapeutic practice of externalizing a person's problem discourse set out to separate the person/client from the problem and/or the restraints that maintained the dominant discourse (problematic stories) about the problem. In Michael White's

therapeutic world, the problem was located outside the person or relationship that had been objectified, identified, and specified (as having the problem), and the problem itself was objectified and given a relational name.

The practice of placing the problem outside the person avoids the fallacy that psychological problems are independent of culture, contexts, and environments.

Part of the creativity of counseling and psychotherapy is creating and assessing credible *alternative contexts* for the client's narratives. Given that clients tell a narrative from their subjective point of view, for example, what other perspective might help? In the following edited example from Freedman and Combs (1996, p. 60), the client is describing her experience of anxiety:

Client: I get this overwhelming feeling of nausea. Not the throw-up nausea . . . My heart starts to beat fast. I mean, I start to sweat.

Therapist: Ok, how does the fear know when it can get you? When it can come in and start creating this overwhelming nausea?

Client: Well, that's an interesting way to pose the question: How does the fear know when it can come and get you?

Therapist: That's how I think of it.

Client: I have to tell you something that's going to sound pretty strange. When you just said that, I was like, oh, it's over there. I almost felt like that . . . Like I felt like some of that shit was kind of lifted out.

In this instance the therapist shifted the context of the problem by referring to the fear as being physically outside, rather than inside, the client. The client then reported feelings of relief and control, because she began to think differently about her anxiety. More specifically, if anxiety were outside her body, the client gained a sense of control over allowing the feeling to get into her body (and her experience).

SHIFT BETWEEN AFFECTIVE EXPERIENCING AND MEANING-MAKING

The research of Pennebaker, Mehl, and Niederhoffer (2003) suggests that emotion-focused processing, by itself, may be insufficient for resolving many clients' problems. Research studies examining the effects of writing about personal traumas typically involve an individual writing, for 15–30 minutes a day from 3–5 days, to create a written narrative of a trauma. Smyth's (1998) meta-analysis of 13 studies compared the written procedure with a control group (typically performing another writing task such as, "Write about your plans for the day"). Similar to the process in individual therapy, participants in the narrative procedure often report an increase in short-term distress before later improvements become evident. Participants evidenced greater benefits if their writing contained (a) more positive emotion words, (b) a moderate number of negative emotion words, and (c) an increase in the number of causal and insight words from the beginning to the end of the narrative. Thus, successful change appears to require that individuals move from a focus on emotions and self to drawing lessons and meanings from the event(s).

This research indicates that for many types of problems, clients should eventually process and experience their emotions as well as their associated cognitions. The client's focus shifts between talking about emotional personal narratives and finding meaning in those narratives. In individual therapy, Anderson (2004, p. 323) notes that more emotion is typically present in the beginning of storytelling—when narrators need to "relinquish an interpretive stance to allow themselves to flow into the story"—with meaning-making occurring later in the process. Rogers combined affect and cognition, defining a feeling "as an emotionally toned experience with ... personal meanings" (Greenberg, Korman, & Paivio, 2001, p. 499).

This weaving between affective experiencing and meaning-making is often not straightforward or predictable, but an ongoing effort that occurs in the "local, embodied nature of therapist–client contact" (McLeod, 2004, p. 362). The therapy process often appears relatively unique to the particular client and therapist working together. With each client the therapist finds the best method to overcome obstacles and facilitate client progress. This implies that the therapist may also avoid certain actions (e.g., advice-giving) that potentially may inhibit the client's ability to focus on meaning-making. The timing and effectiveness of meaning-making significantly depend on the client's progress in becoming aware of and expressing affect around important events and relationships (Hardtke & Angus, 2004). Behavior change may follow from the experience of affect and subsequent meaning-making, or changes in affect and cognition may follow from the client behaving differently in problematic situations.

Client: My father died right before he was going to retire. He had made a lot of plans for what he was going to do with his life and he never got to do any of them.

Therapist: That's sad ... I have a sense that you see this as also applying to you.

> ***Client:*** My children are growing up and there's some sacrifices I made for the family. I'm beginning to think about pursuing some career options that I put on hold.
>
> ***Therapist:*** So you have regrets about some things you didn't do.
>
> ***Client:*** Not really regrets . . . more of a sense that I don't have forever to do what I want to do, and the time may be right soon to change careers.
>
> ***Therapist:*** So one meaning of your father's death is to keep in mind what you want and need, even while you take care of your family and work.
>
> ***Client:*** Yes.
>
> ***Therapist:*** So is there something you need to do now?
>
> ***Client:*** I think I just need to start looking into possibilities for going back to school.

This client has experienced the sadness associated with her father's death, and with the therapist's help, made some sense of the experience. One of the lessons from the experience then leads to an insight about necessary new behaviors, that is, exploring the option of going back to school to start a new career.

Another way to talk about the shifting between emotion and meaning-making is *pacing and leading* (Meier & Davis, 2011; O'Hanlon, 2009). This concept focuses on the timing of the shifting that occurs in therapy. When a therapist *paces* a client, the therapist essentially follows along in terms of the content and affective intensity presented by the client:

> ***Therapist:*** Last week you said that your father passed away two years ago, on this day.
>
> ***Client:*** Yes . . . I've been upset all week.
>
> ***Therapist:*** I can see that you've been crying.

With *leading*, the therapist adds something new to the process. This could involve, for example, a connection that the client had not seen, an increase in the affective intensity of the session, or a shift from emotion to meaning:

Therapist: Last week you said that your father passed away two years ago, on this day.

(pacing)

Client: Yes . . . I've been upset all week.

Therapist: I can see that you've been crying.

(pacing)

Client: Yes . . .

Therapist: I wonder if part of the sadness relates to regrets you've mentioned.

(leading)

Client: Yes . . . my father died right before he was going to retire. He had made a lot of plans for what he was going to do with his life and he never got to do any of them.

Therapist: He made plans he couldn't fulfill.

Client: Yes . . . .

Therapist: This sounds very similar to how you've described your life.

(leading)

Client: Yes . . . there's some sacrifices I made for my job. I've been thinking I want to spend more time with my family.

Therapists generally pace much more than they lead, but the ratio generally depends upon the client's ability to deal with and make sense of new material (Meier & Davis, 2011). Particularly in the beginning of therapy, leading clients into a sensitive area too soon can be risky, as they may drop out if the material becomes too threatening. Therapists lead infrequently in beginning sessions and begin to add new material, staying aware of the client's ability to deal with new directions.

Considerable empirical support exists regarding the benefits of meaning-making. Creating meaning helps to regulate emotion as well as maintain and repair relationships (Singer & Blagov, 2004). Singer and

Blagov's (2004) research with 106 college students, for example, investigated the relationship between *integrative statements* in a written description of a vivid memory with measures of personality adjustment and coping. Integrative statements were those indicative of meaning created, with beginnings such as "I learned that . . ." or "This experience taught me . . . ." Singer and Blagov found that the personality style of moderate self-restraint (but not low or high self-restraint) was associated with a greater number of integrative memories. Singer and Blagov (2004) also reported that meaning-making has been found to be associated with reduced time needed for grieving (Bauer & Bonanno, 2001) and ego development in parents of disabled children (King, Scollon, Ramsey, & May, 2000).

Several strands of research suggest that moving between the client's emotional and cognitive material is important to making therapeutic progress (Angus, Levitt, & Hardtke, 1999; Mergenthaler, 1996). Mergenthaler (1996), for example, investigated the emotional tone and level of reflection of client statements in therapy transcripts. Studying a single case, as well as samples of improved and not improved clients, Mergenthaler found evidence that change in therapy depended upon therapeutic cycles involving key moments, sessions, and time between sessions. These cycles involved shifting between degrees of high and low *emotion* and high and low *abstraction* or *reflection*.

As shown in Figure 3.2, Mergenthaler proposed that these combinations could be represented as four distinct client states. Therapy consists of moving through these states, roughly sequentially: Relaxing, Experiencing, Connecting, Reflecting, and Relaxing again. While discussing a problem, clients first build emotion (often by discussing an event or symptoms), followed by increased reflection (initiated by the therapist or client). Client change and progress in therapy, Mergenthaler reported, requires

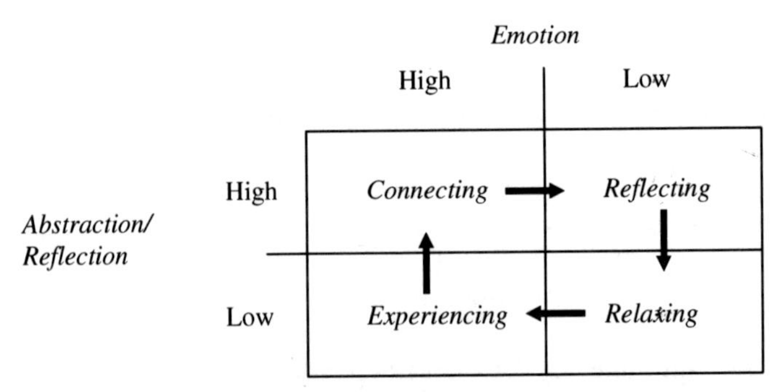

FIGURE 3.2 *Mergenthaler's sequence of affective-cognitive therapy progress.*
Note: *Mergenthaler's research-based depiction of the therapeutic process suggests that most clients move through states of high and low emotional processing and abstraction or reflection.*

one or more Connecting states, where clients reflect on emotional material. However, clients may get stuck in intense emotional states or be hindered by defense mechanisms. Mergenthaler's (1996) analyses of clinical data did find that improved clients evidenced a higher proportion of Connecting states, and fewer Relaxing states, than did clients who did not improve. This trend was also evident over the course of therapy, where improved clients showed increased Connecting states while nonimproving clients did not.

SUMMARY AND IMPLICATIONS

The principles and guidelines offered in this chapter suggest that the therapist pay particular attention to certain forms and characteristics of client stories. From a narrative perspective, the client's self-descriptions, recurring themes and exceptions to those themes, distorted beliefs and descriptions, polarities, and perceived contexts appear particularly important. Content with strong affective attachments is important therapeutic material, and it is the weaving between exploration of affect and related cognitions—often unique to the particular client and therapist—that is a viable path to therapeutic progress. Stiles (2002, p. 357) described this as an *assimilation process* of "recognizing, reformulating, understanding, and eventually resolving" difficult experiences and situations. For many clients, developing a sense of meaning and peacefulness will relate to decreased negative and increased positive affect (cf. Voogt et al., 2005).

Clients approach psychotherapy attempting to solve problems with new solutions or resolve them through meaning-making. For most clients, however, insight alone is not enough for successful change. White and Epston (1990, p. 10) wrote that our lives are "lived experiences," and "to make sense of our lives and to express ourselves, experience must be 'storied' and it is the storying that determines the meaning ascribed to experience." People arrange their experiences of events sequentially, across time, thus providing "a sense of continuity and meaning in their lives" (White & Epston, 1990, p. 10). What is stored in a narrative account becomes the memory of that experience. That memory, however, is only a partial accounting of the lived experience that tends to exclude events that "do not fit with the dominant evolving stories that we and others have about us" (White & Epston, 1990, pp. 11–12).

Samoilov and Goldfried (2000) note that the clinical and research literatures indicate that client symptoms can persist despite evidence of client insight and cognitive self-understanding. Emotional expression and arousal during the processing of client experiences are associated with positive outcomes (Castonguay, Goldfried, Wiser, Raue, & Hayes, 1996; Castonguay, Pincus, Agras, & Hines, 1998; Goldfried, 1979; Greenberg &

Safran, 1984; Hager, 1992; Hayes & Strauss, 1998; Mahoney, 1991; Mohr, Shoham-Solomon, Engle, & Beutler, 1991; Paivio & Greenberg, 1995). Although theorists have employed a variety of descriptions, in essence, humans appear to possess separate but connected emotional and cognitive processing systems. In most people, however, the emotional system appears more able to influence cognitions than vice versa. Given that the cognitive system appears more connected to language than the emotional system, therapists should not assume that the cognitive processing of client stories, independent of an emotional component, will lead to change (cf. Lang, Cuthbert, & Bradley, 1998).

Similarly, affective processing and meaning-making may be insufficient to change client self-descriptions related to personal agency. Clients may avoid situations or fail to persist in the face of obstacles when their assessments of personal competence do not match the perceived demands of specific situations (Bandura, 1977, 1997). To change or adjust these expectations, therapists may need to help clients gain experience with new behaviors, the focus of the next chapter.

Four

Behavioral Elements of Narratives

Narratives can be considered blueprints for action. In client narratives, the key actions typically are behaviors, broadly construed, that the client or others perform. A client, for example, may tell stories about a fight with another student, an argument with a roommate or partner, or poor work or school performance. The emotions and meanings described in client narratives also take place in particular situations, contexts, and environments. Thus, therapists may be able to influence client narratives and self-descriptions through knowledge of and intervention with specific behaviors, situations, and environments.

Of special relevance to efforts to change client self-descriptions are research studies about *self-efficacy*, described in Chapter 3 as an individual's expectations for performing desired behaviors. As shown in Figure 4.1, Bandura (1977, 1997) proposed four sources of self-efficacy: verbal persuasion, physiological arousal, performance accomplishments, and vicarious experience. Verbal persuasion refers to an attempt by one person to convince another that she has the competence to perform the behavior(s) of interest; Bandura (1977) maintained that verbal persuasion is the weakest method for changing self-efficacy expectations. Thus, a therapist may persuade a client in session that one is capable of performing a certain behavior, but it is likely that the increased self-efficacy will not generalize outside the session. Physiological arousal refers to internal states that individuals read as a gauge of their relation to the environment. With high arousal, for example, people may interpret this heightened state as a sign of vulnerability in stressful situations.

In contrast, research indicates that *performance accomplishments* are the strongest method for changing self-efficacy (Bandura, 1997). Changing behavior is the most convincing approach, for most people, of changing their self-image and narratives about themselves in a particular area. As Bandura (1997, p. 80) summarized:

> Enactive mastery experiences are the most influential source of efficacy information because they provide the most authentic

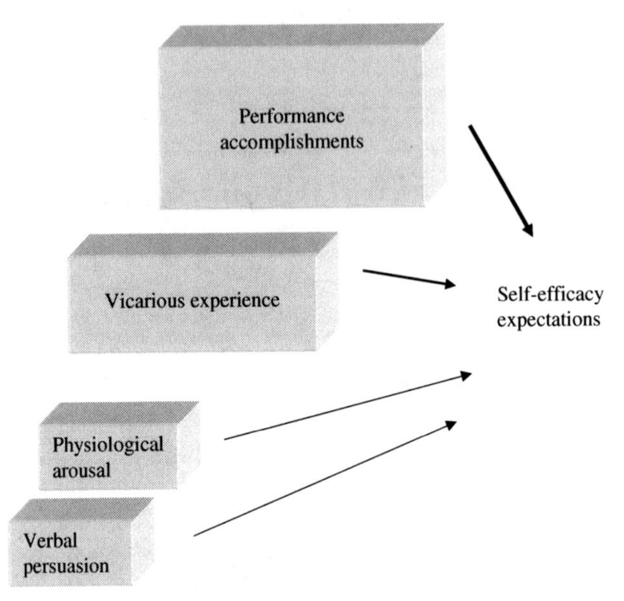

FIGURE 4.1 *Sources of self-efficacy.*
Note: *The size of block illustrates relative impact of sources on self-efficacy. Thus, performance accomplishments are the most powerful influence on a person's self-efficacy, while verbal persuasion by others is the least effective.*

> evidence of whether one can muster whatever it takes to succeed. Successes build a robust belief in one's personal efficacy. Failures undermine it, especially if failures occur before a sense of efficacy is firmly established.

Another powerful source is vicarious experience, which refers to watching others perform a behavior and inferring one's self-efficacy on the basis of the model(s)' performance. Thus, a college student may infer that he may be able to become involved in a romantic relationship when he observes a roommate start and maintain such a relationship. The extent to which one infers self-efficacy from observing others, however, depends on the similarity between model and self (Bandura, 1997). The performance of persons perceived as very dissimilar from oneself, for example, may have little information regarding one's own competencies.

So, a useful path to changing self-descriptions about personal agency is therapeutic effort focused on client behavior and performance. This chapter describes a range of behavior-focused methods that fit with a narrative model.

USE HOMEWORK CREATIVELY

Homework refers to therapeutic activities and behaviors the client performs outside of session. Therapists provide homework for a variety of reasons, but two major purposes are for the client to generalize behavior change from the therapy setting to actual problem situations and test beliefs in real-world settings. Both concepts fit in terms of changing self-descriptions in client narratives.

Rosenthal (2011, p. 10) recommended that homework be kept as simple and brief as possible, that is, "minor, barely noticeable, almost nonexistent, alterations in their behavior." He provided an example of a client who wanted to maintain an exercise program on a stationary bicycle, but had started and stopped the activity many times previously. Instead of the customary 20-minute cycling period on the first day, Rosenthal suggested a strict limit of 15 seconds. The client began this program and ramped up the exercise by small amounts over time. Similarly, a doctoral student who procrastinated about starting his dissertation was given a homework assignment of writing "three mediocre sentences" (Rosenthal, 2011, p. 11). He returned to the next session with 20 pages. In both cases, performing a small behavior helped the client to cope with low self-efficacy for completing the perceived larger task.

Also consider individualizing homework for particular clients. Rosenthal (2011) noted that beginning therapists might develop a few favorite homework assignments because these tasks have proven successful in the past. However, homework should be adapted, customized, and personalized for each client. Homework should be as specific as possible (e.g., concrete goals and behaviors as well as potential obstacles are described), and therapists may provide reminders to complete the homework (e.g., via phone, email, or mail) (L'Abate, 2011).

Perhaps the most important criterion for deciding about a homework assignment is whether the client believes one can do the task (Davis, personal communication, July 1, 2011). That is, it is important for the client to avoid failure with homework and to build self-efficacy for the task in question. This implies that both the client and therapist cooperate to design the assignment and that the client's self-efficacy for the homework task be assessed before the client attempts the task. As per Rosenthal's (2011) examples, the homework task chosen should be one that the client is very likely to be able to complete. The shy client is more likely to successfully initiate a conversation with one fellow student in one week than with 10 fellow students. Similarly, a shy adult who moves into a new neighborhood might first try taking a short walk, gardening in the backyard for 30 minutes, or initiating a 5-minute conversation with a neighbor.

One way to enhance the possibility of success is to ask the client explicitly whether the proposed homework "is something worth trying."

Rather than the therapist persuade the client that she can succeed at some task, it is more useful to adjust or change the task so that the client leaves the session with a sense of competence for performing the behavior in question. In the unlikely event that the client does not successfully perform the task, the failure can be portrayed as a consequence of the task chosen—not the client—and explicitly discussed as such in the next session. The basic philosophy is to produce conditions around the homework that increase the client's self-efficacy for performing the behaviors in question.

Writing about therapy-related topics is also an appropriate homework assignment. As described in Chapter 3, Pennebaker and colleagues' work on writing about trauma has shown that such writing produces a variety of positive effects (Pennebaker et al., 2003; Smyth, 1998). To create a written narrative, participants write about personal traumas for 15–30 minutes a day from 3–5 days. Many therapists ask clients to write as part of their therapy and to discuss their writing when they next come to a session.

CREATE THERAPEUTIC DOCUMENTS

Narrative therapists have outlined methods to create therapeutic documents for use with clients. White and Epston (1990), for example, described the use of letters of invitation to engage individuals reluctant to attend therapy as well as other written documents created with therapeutic intent. Similarly, Madigan (2011, p. 119) described "an international anti-anxiety letter-writing campaign" he organized for Oscar, a 70-year-old man who had been hit by a truck one year earlier. He had recovered from a three-month-long coma and walked again, but reported he had lost all confidence in himself (self-efficacy for daily tasks?) and felt panicky if his wife was not by his side 24 hours a day. Maxine, Oscar's wife, had been organizing all of Oscar's medical care, but wanted to return to her own business. But both their lives had been "taken over by what they both called *anxiety*" (Madigan, 2011, p. 119).

The therapist and client cowrote a letter to client-selected family and community members asking them to write accounts of their current relationship, hopes, and future interactions with Oscar. In the weeks that followed, Oscar brought letters to therapy, with the therapist reading them aloud (because of Oscar's poor eyesight) to Oscar's delight about "his good fortune" regarding the supportive letters (Madigan, 2011, p. 121). Some of the letter writers also came to the session to read their letters to Oscar. Clearly, Oscar benefited from the social support he received via the letters and made an overseas trip that he described as marking his arrival back to health.

Madigan (2011) described the steps in a letter-writing campaign as including identifying people who might see the client as different from the problem description alone (e.g., as *anxious*). This identification process might include assistance from significant others such as a partner or friends in attendance. The therapist or agency might provide financial assistance if needed, in terms of stamps and envelopes, and the therapist's office employed as the return address if privacy is an issue. Contacted persons are invited to the therapy session to read the letter, if possible, and the client keeps the collected letters as a way to review information about her- or himself. More details about therapeutic letters are available in Madigan (2011), and White and Epston (1990) contains information about other therapeutic letters. Also see Alberti (2011) for a similar letter enlisting the help of others for clients in assertiveness training.

Therapists are also just beginning to explore how to use websites, email, and other electronic communication to facilitate therapeutic work. These newer methods may complement journaling, where clients regularly write about personal issues and their reactions to them (Progoff, 1992). All the documents produced by therapists and clients have the added potential to function as assessment data. A therapist's summary letter of the changes made by a client can document progress and outcome for the client, an insurance company, or other interested parties.

ROLE-PLAY DIFFICULT ASPECTS OF CLIENT NARRATIVES

Role-play refers to the playing or acting of parts of a clinically relevant story. The purpose is typically to assess client behaviors and self-efficacy, impart new skills, and practice and learn new behaviors (Egan, 2001; Ivey, 2002). Here, the client is not simply telling the problem-focused story, but acting it out in the presence of the therapist or therapy group. In clinical training, role-playing is employed to teach interviewing (e.g., open-ended questions), listening (e.g., reflection of feelings), and diagnostic skills (e.g., with standardized patients) (Barney & Shea, 2007). In both settings, role-plays offer a number of benefits:

1. Role-plays can be created for the client's specific problematic situation (typically an interaction with another person).
2. To the extent that the specifics of role-plays mirror the problematic situation, role-plays allow assessment of the client's behavioral skills, cognitions such as self-efficacy for particular tasks, and emotional reactions in that situation.
3. Talking about the required behaviors before, during, and after the role-play enables an assessment of the client's conceptualization and understanding of the situation. In addition to the conclusion, the role-play can be stopped at any point to assess the client's understanding and provide feedback.

4. The complexity and difficulty of role-plays can be matched to the challenges the client faces in the problematic situation(s).
5. Mistakes can be encouraged, accepted, and corrected in the safe setting of the therapy session. The therapist can react realistically when the client performs poorly in a role-play, but feedback is provided in the spirit of helping the client. Practice can be continued until the desired level of performance occurs.
6. Therapist and client can switch roles, allowing the therapist to model the performance of desired behaviors.

Standardized problem situations, typically focused on assertive behavior, have been described in the literature for clients with social interaction difficulties (e.g., Kern, 1991; Krumboltz & Thoresen, 1976). If feasible, audio- or videotaping the role-plays allows for additional feedback to the client about her or his performance and methods of improvement. Overall, role-plays offer a method of increasing the client's self-efficacy through performance accomplishments, the most powerful source of personal competence (Bandura, 1977).

Krumboltz and Thoresen (1976) described the use of role-play with a client named Joan, a 45-year-old woman, separated from her husband and living with her three children and elderly mother. Returning to work part-time and college study part-time, Joan complained about her domineering, critical mother, who nevertheless provided important help with housework, money, and babysitting. The therapist worked with Joan to elicit specific information to write a script for a role-play where Joan could learn and try out new behaviors. Here are condensed excerpts from Krumboltz and Thoresen (1976, pp. 470–474):

> ***Therapist:*** First, *describe* to me what she is doing when she tells you what church to go to.
>
> ***Joan:*** She just starts hassling me—leading my life.
>
> ***Therapist:*** *How* is she hassling, leading your life? Specifically, what is she saying?
>
> ***Joan:*** She says she doesn't want me to go to the church I'm going to.
>
> ***Therapist:*** Does she say something like this: "Joan, you shouldn't go to that church because it is too far away and you're wasting gas?"
>
> ***Joan:*** Yes, that's it.

. . .

Therapist: Let's just talk about how you feel when she brings up the subject of church going. If you were going to tell your mother how helpless and depressed you feel every time she brings up this subject, what would you say to her?

Joan: It makes me angry—like I'm a little kid who can't make my own decisions when I'm really an adult.

. . .

Therapist: One last step is to stipulate consequences for her.

Joan: That's the problem. I can't do anything with her.

Therapist: You do something now. You throw cups and slam doors.

Joan: But it's impossible to get through to her. What can I do?

Therapist: Just fantasize for a moment. What would you *like* to do?

Joan: I'd like to walk *calmly* out of the room the first time she mentions church going!

Joan and her therapist continued to work on what they termed an "assertiveness script." Joan wrote the final version and then learned her lines; the therapist and client then tape-recorded the scene. With therapist feedback about how to improve her nonverbals, Joan and her therapist continued to record the scene and listen to it. For homework, Joan also practiced her lines in a front of a bathroom mirror at home. The therapist and client continued to work on role-plays, with the therapist improvising more difficult situations for Joan. Four years after the conclusion of the therapy, the therapist sent a letter to Joan seeking information about her perception of the therapy. Joan identified role-playing in front of a mirror as particularly helpful since she could hear her voice aloud.

USE CLIENT NONVERBAL BEHAVIORS TO INCREASE CLIENT SELF-UNDERSTANDING

Nonverbal behaviors are ways people convey information independent of speech content. These observable behaviors include hand gestures, facial expressions, body posture, tone of voice, eye contact, and body motion. Therapists typically trust *nonverbal communication* as more indicative of basic feelings because, for most people, censoring verbal communication is easier than controlling nonverbals (Meier & Davis, 2011). Depending on the client and the stage of therapy, therapists may help clients become aware of the nonverbal level as a way of deepening self-understanding.

Gestalt therapists tend to be very focused and skilled in working with clients' nonverbals. The following is a brief transcript from a video of Fritz Perls demonstrating Gestalt therapy with a client named Gloria, part of the training videos noted in Chapter 2 (Shostrom, 1966):

> ***Perls:*** We are going to interview for half an hour.
>
> ***Gloria:*** Right away I'm scared.
>
> ***Perls:*** You say you're scared but you're smiling. I don't understand how one can be scared and smile at the same time.
>
> ***Gloria:*** And I'm also suspicious of you; I think you understand very well. I think you know that when I get scared I laugh or I kid to cover up.
>
> ***Perls:*** You do have stage fright.
>
> ***Gloria:*** Um, I don't know. I'm mostly aware of you, I'm afraid that—I'm afraid you'll have such a direct attack that you're going to get me in the corner and I'm afraid of it. I want you to be more on my side.
>
> ***Perls:*** You say get me in your corner and you put your hand on your chest. Is this your corner?
>
> ***Gloria:*** Well, it's like—Yeah, it's like I'm afraid, you know.
>
> ***Perls:*** Where would you like to go? Can you describe the corner you'd like to go to?
>
> ***Gloria:*** Yeah, it's back in a corner, where I'm completely protected.
>
> ***Perls:*** And there you would be safer from me.
>
> ***Gloria:*** Well, I know I wouldn't really... But, it feels safer, yes.

Perls: You made your way to this corner, you're perfectly safe now. What would you do in this corner?

Perls attempted to help Gloria become aware of her personal strengths by drawing attention to her nonverbals. Perls focused Gloria on her smile, for example, even when she professed to feeling afraid. He also talked about how she would feel if she could retreat to a "corner," where she could take refuge from Perls. In essence, Perls refocused Gloria's awareness of her feelings by pointing out her nonverbals and her description of a metaphorical place to hide from him. Related Gestalt techniques that have been adopted by therapists with other theoretical orientations include the empty-chair and two-chair techniques.

PAY ATTENTION TO CLIENT AND THERAPIST VERBAL BEHAVIORS

Holzer, Mergenthaler, Pokorny, Kachele, and Luborsky (1996) studied the verbal behaviors of therapists and clients in the Penn Psychotherapy Project. They examined 80 transcripts of the most and least improved outpatient clients who received psychodynamic psychotherapy provided by male residents. Holzer et al. (1996) found that for patients who improved, therapists talked more in the beginning of therapy and less as the therapy progresses. For patients who showed the least improvement, therapists talked more as therapy progressed; for patients who failed to improve, more talkative patients showed the least improvement. The picture that emerges from this research is that the therapist is more active in the beginning of therapy and gradually relinquishes the stage to the client, who becomes more verbally active over time. This makes sense, as the therapist typically spends more time, in early sessions, gaining clinical information and setting the stage for an intervention. Clients who talk a great deal in therapy may be using talk as *resistance*, given that they typically are not processing affect and meaning-making as needed to make therapeutic progress.

The results of studies examining the effects of writing about traumatic experiences are comparable to psychotherapy research findings (Smyth, 1998); these studies also have potential implications for how narrative-based therapies could be conducted. Healthy writing is associated with a high number of self-references on some days but not on others. Pennebaker et al. (2003, p. 569) concluded that "people who always write in a particular voice—such as first person singular—simply do not improve." This finding suggests that successful clients learn how to shift back and forth between their personal perspective and an empathic view of others' outlook. This research also suggests that pronoun use may be a useful indicator of the speaker's modeling of social interactions. Pennebaker et al. (2003, p. 570) wrote that:

> To use a pronoun requires the speaker and listener to share a common knowledge of who the referent is ... Pronoun use requires a relatively sophisticated awareness of the audience's ability to track who is who.

Campbell and Pennebaker (2003, p. 64) also concluded that "individuals who altered their individual and social perspectives from day to day were the participants most likely to benefit from the disclosure exercise."

Writers were also more likely to benefit if their text contained more positive emotion words, a moderate number of negative emotion words, and an increasing number of causal and insight words from the beginning to the conclusion of writing (Pennebaker et al., 2003). Writing participants evidenced an increase in short-term distress before later improvements occurred, and Smyth's (1998) review also found that larger gains were evident for men and when writing periods were spread out over a longer time period.

USE THE CASE CONCEPTUALIZATION AS AN INTERVENTION

Case conceptualization refers to the selection and depiction of the key elements of a client's presenting problems, psychological functioning, and treatment plans (Meier, 2003). It is a clinical, and sometimes scientifically-based, narrative about the important causes of the client's problems and how best to intervene with those causes. Clinical researchers such as Layden, Newman, Freeman, and Morse (1993) and Needleman (1999) have argued that case conceptualization can help clinicians organize and make sense of the overwhelming number of details present in any case.

When the conceptualization is shared with clients, it functions as an intervention that can help clients to understand and reduce the seeming complexity of their problems, and subsequently increase their motivation for treatment. Sharing the conceptualization with the client can also increase confidence in the therapist, expectations for positive change, and openness to methods derived from the conceptualization, particularly when clients see that their therapist has a sophisticated understanding of them (Meier, 2003).

While clinical researchers have proposed a variety of formats and content for case conceptualizations (Beck, Emery, & Greenberg, 2005; Berman, 1997; Eells, 1997; Lambert, 1994; Mash & Hunsley, 1993), one basic approach is to simply describe important process and outcome elements for a client (Meier, 2003). *Process* refers to causes, that is, the factors influencing client problems, while *outcomes* refers to effects, the problems that result from the causative processes. Desired outcomes are clinical *goals; objectives* are intermediate steps necessary to reach longer-term goals (Jongsma & Peterson, 1995; Wiger, 1999). A client *model* is the clinician's explicit representation of process and outcome elements for a particular individual.

In the case of a client (see below) who presents with social phobia and shyness, for example, the process element can be conceptualized as a series of interpersonal conflicts (e.g., his mother pressuring him to be more social) that lead to a current outcome, his vaguely described distress. The therapist suggests that a goal of therapy is to learn assertiveness skills, which includes learning how to share one's feelings with others, particularly in conflict situations. One possible intermediate objective would be for the client to be able to express his feelings to the therapist before eventually generalizing this behavior outside of the therapy session. A graphic model of this client's processes, outcomes, objectives, and goal is presented in Figure 4.2.

Therapists may wish to codevelop the case conceptualization with clients. That is, the conceptualization is a kind of story and the client's perspective on this story is important. In the example below (based on a role-play about a social phobic, at http://www.youtube.com/watch?v=7O45nSwxDJ8&feature=fvw), the therapist used the client's statements to conceptualize that increased assertiveness could be an important goal in therapy.

> ***Client:*** I want to try to be more sociable, but I do enjoy spending time by myself. I guess, I need to try to be more outgoing and, I guess, try to make more friends, but, I mean, maybe my mom is right. What kind of loser hardly has any friends and never leaves his dorm room?
>
> ***Therapist:*** You seem stuck between trying to be more sociable and being okay with spending lots of time by yourself.
>
> ***Client:*** My mom wants me to be more outgoing and to do more things, I guess like my brother. He's always been sociable and popular and . . . I don't know, it's just hard to compete with that or to think that I need to show the same personality. But I mean . . . I don't know, it's hard for me to do that sort of thing. I just want to tell my mom I'm not Jason, you know, I'm not going . . . I probably can't be like that.
>
> ***Therapist:*** As you talk about your problems, my sense is you have trouble being assertive with other people.

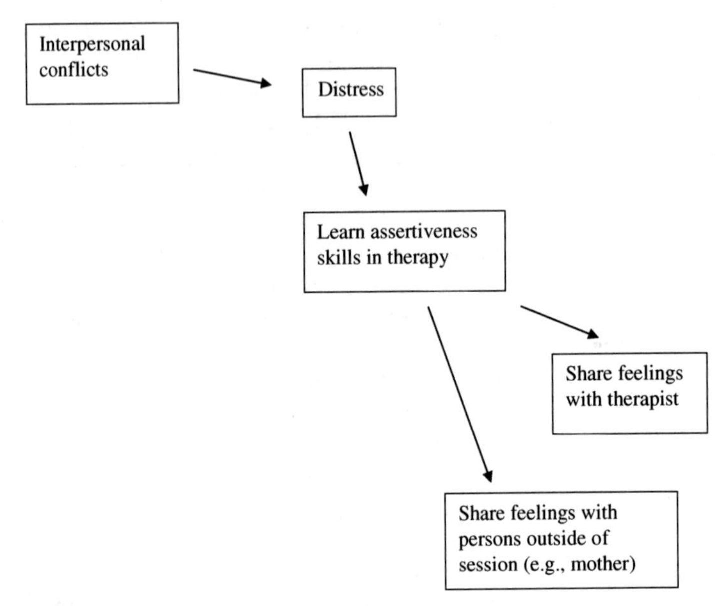

FIGURE 4.2 *Example of a client model.*
Note: *For a person who presents with social phobia and shyness, a goal of therapy may be to learn assertiveness skills, which includes sharing one's feelings with others, particularly in conflict situations that lead to distress. One possible intermediate objective would be for the client to be able to express his feelings to the therapist before eventually generalizing this behavior outside of the therapy session.*

Client: What do you mean?

Therapist: You have trouble talking about yourself and your feelings to other people. You said you don't really want to be here, in counseling, but your roommate insisted. You want to tell your mother you can't be like your brother, but you haven't done that.

Client: Yes.

Therapist: So it may make some sense to think about helping you learn to be more assertive with other people.

Client: Ok, how can I be more assertive?

Several cautions apply to sharing a conceptualization with clients. Since sharing or co-creating a conceptualization with a client can be considered an intervention, the timing of this activity is important. As with any intervention, sharing a conceptualization too early, for a particular client, may be ineffective or confusing. Berman (1997) noted that some clients may be unable to understand sophisticated concepts from certain therapeutic perspectives; they may benefit from explanations related to the concepts in the conceptualization (Berman, 1997). Metaphors may be useful for translating elements of the case conceptualization. With a depressed client, for example, the broken leg metaphor (i.e., a broken leg takes time to heal and may hurt more in the beginning) may be a useful way of explaining the need to discuss painful experiences over a period of time (i.e., therapeutic processes). Caution is also due with intellectualizing clients who may latch onto the conceptualization as a means of resisting further work. Such a client, for example, may try to engage the therapist in a debate about the conceptualization or spend an inordinate amount of time researching the conceptualization or diagnosis.

LEARN AND UNDERSTAND THE CLIENT'S PROBLEM-RELATED CONTEXT(S)

A narrative therapies (NTs) approach is probably most different from a medical model that places the client's problem within the person and the person's biochemistry. At its most simplistic depiction, in the medical model, a mental health professional might conduct an intake interview and then assign a client a *Diagnostic and Statistical Manual of Mental Disorders* (*DSM*; American Psychiatric Association, 2000) diagnosis of anxiety or depression; the problem is then often treated with medication. From an NT perspective, no problem occurs independently of a person's contexts. These include political, familial, cultural, gender, school, work, race/ethnicity, sexuality, and religious contexts.

These contexts become an issue when a person runs into conflicts because of their interactions in one or more domains: a gay person who wants to marry and adopt a child in a place where that is illegal; a Black school child is disciplined differently than a White student in a school system with few students of color; a female student decides not to pursue a particular vocation because her parents view it as only appropriate for boys. All of these individuals might present to a therapist with anxiety or depression; while medication might mitigate their symptoms, it would not address the long-term causes that are situational in nature.

Lafrance and Stoppard (2007) discuss how a cultural narrative about what constitutes a "good woman" can cause and maintain depression in women. Statements by research participants are listed below (Lafrance & Stoppard, 2007, p. 27). What context(s) do these women perceive?

Client: I try to become this super person that does everything, and I feel guilty for not doing it. And I think it still goes back to just wanting to make sure they are happy with me, that I am a good person.

Client: So maybe that one week a month, I am going to scream and yell at my kids. And then I thought, well maybe I should never have had children, maybe I just am not a good mother.

Client: But at times it's like, you know, everything seems to be so couple oriented, and if you don't have kids and you don't have a family, there is something wrong with you, especially when you are 29 and 30 years old.

Lafrance and Stoppard's (2007) research with depressed women indicated that these women's daily lives are "consumed by domestic practices and governed by the needs of others" (p. 26).

CHANGE SELF-DESCRIPTIONS WITH EXPOSURE TO FEARED SITUATIONS

A key question for many clients is, what is necessary to change the core beliefs and themes in personal narratives? While much of the discussion in the previous chapters involved the client experiencing affect in session while relating a narrative, research on exposure therapies demonstrates that clients generally benefit more when the experience is *in vivo* (Craske, 1999). Heightened arousal is part of the answer, but heightened arousal may be a natural consequence of the individual being placed in what they perceive as an anxiety-provoking situation.

One of the most effective ways to change clients' self-descriptions in personal narratives is to help them change their problem behaviors. Barlow (1988) suggests that clients act their way into feeling differently. As indicated by Bandura's (1977, 1997) self-efficacy theory, performance accomplishments provide the most credible source of information about expectations of personal competence. For clients who *disproportionately* experience fear, anxiety, and other NA in particular situations, exposure to these situations may be the most powerful intervention for change. For exposure to be successful, Linehan (1993) described several conditions that should be present:

1. The client reexperiences the problem situation in such a way that the problematic behaviors, thoughts, and/or feelings occur. To do so, the client can enter the actual problem-provoking situation,

or talk about the situation. A major issue here is determining how intense the initial exposure experiences should be. Weg (2011) indicated that this decision is essentially the client's. Particularly if the client reports initial apprehension about an exposure task, the therapist's question (Weg, 2011, p. 41) is, "Ok, if you can't do *that*, what *can* you do?"

2. The client's affective response is not reinforced. That is, the exposure situation contains information that has the capacity to correct the client's overreactions (Foa & Kozak, 1986). One therapist tried to expose a client with a fear of driving over bridges by accompanying the client while they drove back and forth over a bridge. The therapist was surprised that the client continued to experience considerable anxiety despite the exposure. When the therapist inquired what the client was experiencing on the bridge, he replied, "I'm thinking this bridge is going to collapse and we'll die." The therapist had provided the eliciting situation as described in #1, but failed to provide a method for correcting the client's catastrophic thoughts (e.g., "Notice that as we drive across the bridge, it is not collapsing"). As Linehan (1993) emphasized, the therapist must provide a new, corrective account in the overreaction situation.
3. Maladaptive coping responses cannot occur (e.g., the client cannot decrease anxiety by escaping the situation). When clients have the ability to escape the problematic situation, they "avoid emotional cues and inhibit the experience of emotions; thus, they have no opportunity to learn that when unfettered, emotions come and go" (Linehan, 1993, p. 345). Emotions can be compared to the wind: They naturally ebb and flow unless the individual attempts to avoid them. Linehan (1993, p. 351) emphasized that the therapist's message is that "the only way out of emotions is through them."
4. The individual learns to gain a sense of acceptance and control over the situation and herself/himself. This increases self-efficacy for particular tasks.
5. The exposure lasts long enough and is practiced frequently enough for the beneficial effects to occur and persist over time. Linehan's (1993) reading of the research literature indicated that exposure has to be intense enough to elicit the overreaction, but does not need to be extreme; graduated exposure is easier for clients and is effective. The client should end the exposure and the emotion should evidence some decrease in intensity before exposure is ended.

Linehan (1993) also noted that exposure may also be effective for clients who have trouble with any NA states, including panic, shame, sadness, and anxiety.

Placing clients in actual situations and environments may be impractical in many clinical settings, but clinicians should be creative and willing to utilize available resources; this includes holding sessions in problematic environments rather than in an office. If the client's affect and problems center on another person or family, then couples counseling or family counseling is likely to be most appropriate if feasible. Similarly, persons with interpersonal issues may be most likely to benefit from group therapy if they are willing to experience this modality.

An advanced graduate student was treating a client who had been in an automobile accident and in constant pain in the months since the accident. The client had quit her job and become agoraphobic. She reported becoming very agitated around other people and consequently avoided all social contact, even with previously close friends. At the beginning of one session, the client reported that she had forgotten to purchase the tea she usually drank during the session. The therapist agreed to walk down to a coffee shop in the same building with the client while she purchased her tea. However, when they arrived at the shop, there was a long line of people, which agitated the client, who nevertheless wanted something to drink. So the therapist and client waited in line, talking quietly about what the client was experiencing and how she might tolerate her feelings during the 10-minute wait.

The client did finish this unintentional social exposure period and upon returning to the therapist's office spoke with the therapist about the ordeal. With the therapist's assistance, the client had done some deep breathing to help her through the social exposure. The 10-minute exposure and subsequent discussion with her therapist appeared to change the client's willingness to engage with other people, as she proceeded in the next weeks to reengage with her friends in social events despite some continued anxiety. The student therapist continued this *in vivo* exposure at the start of subsequent sessions to maintain and extend the procedure's benefits.

CHANGE SOCIAL ENVIRONMENTS

Social and physical environments exert strong influences on human behavior, and individuals also change the environments in which they live (Bandura, 1986; Wachtel, 1973). Social scientists have theorized and studied person–environment interactions for many decades (e.g., Lewin, 1935; Murray, 1938, cited in McFall & McDonel, 1986). For therapists, these concepts allow shifting of the focus of intervention to the social environments in which clients live. That means intervening, for example, with families, couples, work organizations, and schools; for many narrative therapists, it also means paying attention to issues of *social justice*.

Family therapy fits well with narrative approaches in terms of both foundational philosophies and intervention approaches (Meier & Davis, 2011). Philosophically, family therapists do not see individuals' problems as residing solely within the individual client (i.e., the *identified patient*), but as relating to the social systems to which clients belong, the most important of which is often the family (deShazer, 1982; Minuchin, 1974). In family therapy, many therapists employ a systems approach where the therapist first identifies the communication patterns of family members (Ng, 1999; Satir, 1988). On this basis, the therapist helps the family members change maladaptive interactions so that a new structure of communication and interaction takes hold. For example, families often act to preserve their status quo and avoid dealing with serious problems such as conflict between husband and wife (Goldenberg & Goldenberg, 1995). In some families, this means that the family environment is set up to deflect attention from such problems by scapegoating one or more family member as bad and symptomatic.

Schools are another social environment with a powerful effect on their inhabitants. With many children and adolescents, interactions with fellow students, as well as teachers and other adults, may be as influential as those with family members. Consequently, school-based conflicts ranging from bullying to poor academic performance bring many children and adolescents into therapy, and intervening in school situations may provide considerable benefits. Figure 4.3 contains an example of a therapeutic letter sent by a therapist to a young client's school principal (Madigan, 2011); the letter can be read as an attempt to change the social perceptions of the client at his school. That is, the therapist disagrees with the assignment of anger management training to the client and indicates that the client is a victim of racial injustice at the school.

Social justice is a useful rubric for considering all of the social contexts that influence human rights in relation to psychotherapy (Speight & Vera, 2001). For example, are mental health services a basic right for all people? For-profit models now drive both private (insurance) and public (government) funding agencies for mental health agencies (Davis & Meier, 2001; Madigan, 2011). While it is possible in theory to integrate managed care methods into mental health practice, the drive for profits by private insurers and the push to make vulnerable individuals pay for more of their mental health services has, to date, largely been a disaster for many persons seeking psychotherapy (Davis & Meier, 2001). The implementation of managed care methods has resulted in severe limits on number of sessions in many settings, increased administrative paperwork for therapists, restrictions on who may provide services, and pressure to conclude psychotherapy prematurely.

Dear Mr. X,

My name is [therapist]. I am a therapist who had the pleasure of talking with one of your students, Jessie, and his mother last week.

The reason I am writing is to discuss my concerns regarding the school's participation in events this past fall that have placed Jessie's reputation as a good student, friend, and son in a certain kind of danger. To begin with, it is very clear to me that Jessie does not need anger management treatment.

My primary concern at this time is Jessie's future reputation as a student in your school program. My fear is that the fugitive reputation the court has given him is unjust and that this unjust reputation will be written into his school file...

As a principal, you have certainly experienced how difficult it can be for some students to live down a bad reputation. Jessie has done little to deserve the harsh personal and financial punishment he received, and I believe that other factors such as race, social status, and class may have influenced his sentence.

I would appreciate a time set aside to talk to you about these concerns.

Sincerely,

[therapist]

FIGURE 4.3 *Example of a therapeutic letter.*

SUMMARY AND IMPLICATIONS

Issues around personal agency are implicit or explicit themes of many client narratives. The focus of this chapter has been on the use of behavioral experiences to help clients change self-descriptions in clinical narratives. Self-efficacy theory (Bandura, 1977, 1997) provides a useful description for helping clients learn to increase their expectations of personal competence through performance accomplishments and other means. Homework, role-plays, and exposure to feared situations were among the methods described to help clients gain performance accomplishments. In addition, behavioral methods have demonstrated the benefits of collecting data regarding clients' progress and outcomes. These include providing feedback to therapists and clients so that corrective actions can be taken when clients fail to progress in therapy. Feedback also provides documentation of progress and change to interested parties such as schools, parents, and insurance companies. Chapter 6 describes a variety of assessment methods useful for such purposes.

Feldman, Bruner, Renderer, and Spitzer (1990) noted that narratives tend to describe stories in terms of actions *or* the self-perceived experiences of the actors. Psychotherapy theories often focus on one or the other end of this continuum (e.g., behavior therapy versus client-centered therapy), but an emphasis on language and narratives that grounds change in affect, meaning-making, *and* new behaviors offers a useful integration of these divergent approaches.

Five

Obstacles to Therapeutic Progress

Most clients must cope with intense negative affect (NA), recurring thoughts, and avoidance behaviors that accompany the problems and issues that bring them into therapy. Clients naturally try to avoid these NA states, thoughts, and situations, and consequently become stuck, regress, or are unable to comply with or benefit from therapeutic interventions. In behavior therapy terms, *avoidance behaviors* maintain anxiety by keeping the individual from exposure and eventual habituation to actually safe or manageable situations (Campbell-Sills & Barlow, 2007; Moses & Barlow, 2006).

From a narrative and language perspective, both client and therapist can introduce obstacles into the therapeutic process. Obstacles are frequently related to aspects of lived experiences that have been *excluded* from narratives, including:

1. Being *unaware of* or *resistant to experiencing* strong NA and associated thoughts and behaviors described in client narratives.
2. Being unwilling to *talk about* strong NA and associated states. That is, either clients or therapists may be motivated to avoid sharing, exploring, or processing difficult aspects of their stories.

Clients may be very reluctant to share strong feelings because they do not expect relief, may be ashamed to reveal secrets or admit failure, expect to be critically judged, or fear losing control (Teyber & McClure, 2011). Research indicates that clients may omit important content in session because, among other reasons, the material feels emotionally overwhelming (Hill, Thompson, Cogar, & Denman, 1993). For many clients, sharing narratives with strong NA can be psychologically comparable to opening a door to a room full of flames.

Avoidance of emotion may also be a strategy employed by individuals in particular situations, including cultural and occupational settings. Studying a sample of Army soldiers who returned from a 12-month tour in Iraq, Bliese et al. (2007) assessed symptoms related to posttraumatic stress disorder, depression, anger, relationship problems, and general psychological distress in 509 randomly selected soldiers who provided data at immediate postdeployment and 120 days later. Bliese et al. (2007) found that prevalence rates for most mental health problems were two to five times higher at 120 days postdeployment than at immediate postdeployment. Milliken et al. (2007) essentially replicated these results in a large sample of soldiers returning from Iraq who evidenced more mental health problems six months after return than at their immediate postdeployment. Similarly, Sigmon et al. (2005) found evidence that men, compared to women, tend to underreport symptoms of depression.

Strong affect can also be a problem for therapists. As Pierce, Nichols, and Dubrin (1983, p. xiii) noted, "psychotherapists all too often respond to painful feelings by trying to ignore, analyze, or block them." Research and clinical experience suggests that at times, even experienced therapists may avoid addressing clients' sensitive and strong NA (Hill & O'Brien, 1999; Teyber & McClure, 2011). Therapists' emotional states, their inexperience with strong NA, and their feelings of responsibility for causing or resolving strong emotion problems may influence their ability to be open and accepting of clients' feelings. Therapists can also hinder the client's sharing of therapeutic material through such acts as talking too much, giving advice, and premature problem solving (Meier & Davis, 2011).

This chapter addresses these obstacles to therapeutic progress, as introduced by both client and therapist. Client issues are typically more prevalent and are addressed first.

CLIENT ISSUES

This half of the chapter focuses on obstacles to clinical progress related to affect, thoughts, and behaviors in clients' narratives. Progress in therapy is seldom a linear process. Mergenthaler's (1996) model of therapy progress indicates that clients typically cycle through more or less intense reflection and emotional experiencing. As described below, lack of progress for many clients often centers on issues with strong NA associated with rumination and avoidant behavior.

Help Clients Explore Difficult Affect, Thoughts, and Situations

Most therapists, after gaining some clinical experience and training, can recognize their client's most intense affect. Client *resistance* can arise, however, when the therapist discusses intense affect when the client is not yet ready to do so, and becomes self-protective. Rather than directly address that intense affect with an avoidant client, one alternative is to employ techniques such as *open-ended questions* with clients around their affect. This allows the client to choose (albeit unconsciously, in some instances) what level of affective intensity they are able to tolerate. Teyber and McClure (2011, p. 193) suggested the following questions:

1. What are you feeling now?
2. Can you tell me more about that feeling?
3. How do you feel as you tell me about ____?
4. Help me understand what you are feeling as you tell me this.

Client: My father died about six months ago and I just don't feeling anything.

Therapist: What was your relationship like with him?

Client: We lived in different cities, but we talked every day on the phone.

Therapist: He was an important person in your life.

Client: Yeah ... He wanted to turn the family business over to me. I went to law school but haven't found a job. He thought if I took over his business, I'd have a good job and someone would keep the business going.

Therapist: But something about that bothered you?

Client: Yeah, I don't know.

Therapist: What are you feeling now?

Client: Stressed.

Therapist: Can you tell me more about that feeling?

Client: Yeah ... I was so happy by the idea of finally having a job where I could make a living. But then ... I would have failed as a lawyer.

Therapist: Those are strong feelings to sort out, positive and negative. I can understand how it might feel overwhelming at times.

Client: Definitely.

Therapist: Well, this is a good place to begin to talk about these feelings.

Client: Ok.

The therapist can stay at the affective intensity level chosen by the client. In effect, the therapist is pacing the client's affective intensity, instead of the more common practice of mirroring the client's content. This becomes a starting point for *immediacy* in the therapeutic relationship: The client can express and experience some level of emotion, in the presence of the therapist (Teyber & McClure, 2011).

A client's *cultural background* may also be a source of resistance for exploring sensitive areas. Zhong (2008) discussed culturally sensitive ways of providing psychotherapy for traditional Chinese individuals who may be reluctant to express affect in social situations such as therapy. Zhong recommended the incorporation of Chinese proverbs into therapy so that difficult psychological issues could be indirectly discussed and thereby reduce embarrassment and hurt. For a client who is too passive, for example, a proverb such as "Waiting under the tree to catch a rabbit" can communicate the idea without the client experiencing the statement as criticism. Zhong (2008) provided a set of proverbs that may be useful for clinical issues, including somatization, poor problem solving, and persistence in the face of difficult problems. Polkinghorne (2004) and McLeod (1997) also provide information about culturally sensitive ways of dealing with obstacles in therapy.

Reinforce When a Client Shares Intense Negative Affect

Whatever the corresponding language of your theoretical orientation, it can be important to acknowledge and debrief when a client does share an intense feeling with the therapist. Most importantly, such responses should be genuine (Teyber & McClure, 2011).

Therapist: So telling someone else about this feeling would be a danger to your family?

Client: No, it would be a betrayal.

Therapist: How so?

Client: It would be embarrassing for people to know that I feel this way.

Therapist: Including your therapist?

Client: Well . . . probably not. It's more like, neighbors or family friends.

Therapist: Thank you for helping me understand your concerns about sharing this.

Client: Sure . . . I didn't really understand why I couldn't tell you.

And this is an example from Teyber and McClure (2011, p. 199), about a woman who allowed her boyfriend to again move back in with her:

Client: Don't you think I'm most pathetic for letting this jerk move back in with me again?

Therapist: No, I don't see you as pathetic or weak. But I do see your sadness right now and how much all of this has hurt you. I think you are showing great courage in sharing this with me; and I see how hard you are trying to sort out what you need and want—I respect that.

Here the therapist acknowledges the difficult task the client has accomplished in the sharing of what she perceived as a shameful act. The therapist accepted what she did at face value, pointed out her sadness, and labeled her act of sharing this incident as "courageous."

One of the most reinforcing actions a therapist can perform is validating the client's affect (Linehan, 1993). As shown in the dialog below, the validation should be genuine and empathic (adapted from Teyber & McClure, 2011, pp. 203–204):

Client: I told my parents how scared I've been after being mugged, but they . . . I don't know . . . I was hoping for something different from them.

Therapist: That makes sense, you needed to be heard, your fears acknowledged, rather than hear about them and their problems.

Client: That's exactly what I wanted—them to have just listened to me, to my needs, given me the feeling that I could come to them, have a need, and not always seem so much in control.

Therapist: You are putting it so well. You know, here with me, you can say exactly what you need. It makes sense to me that you were afraid. Being mugged would make most people really afraid.

Wanting to be heard and responded to by your parents makes a lot of sense to me.

Collaborate With the Client to Learn the Threat Associated With an Intense Feeling

Teyber and McClure (2011) proposed that rather than push for the client to share intense feelings (of which experienced therapists are often already aware), the therapist should focus on the process or factor that is inhibiting the disclosure. So the therapist may ask the client, for example, about what is stopping the client from self-disclosing affect, how revealing the feeling might influence the therapeutic relationship or other relationships, or what the danger might be in experiencing or revealing the feeling.

Therapist: What's stopping you from sharing this strong feeling?

Client: Well . . . I feel like I'm revealing a family secret.

Therapist: A family secret, when this is *your* feeling?

Client: In my family we keep this kind of feeling in the family. We don't tell other people.

Therapist: So telling someone else about this feeling would be a danger to your family?

Client: No, it would be a betrayal.

Therapist: How so?

Client: It would be embarrassing for people to know that I feel this way.

Therapist: Including your therapist?

Client: Well . . . probably not. It's more like, neighbors or family friends.

Therapist: Thank you for helping me to understand your concerns about sharing this.

Client: Sure . . . it wasn't too clear to me why I felt like I couldn't tell you.

> ***Therapist:*** It sounds like this kind of feeling would be an embarrassment that might be shared with others, if it got outside the family.
>
> ***Client:*** Yes.
>
> ***Therapist:*** But that can't happen here.

In this example the client becomes aware of what is stopping him from sharing the feeling with anyone else, including the therapist. It is almost as if his family has created an invisible fence so that strong feelings cannot escape.

Clients can be uncomfortable with their own thoughts and feelings. In the dialog (adapted from Rae, 2008, p. 75) below, the therapist (a) accepts the client's resistance to talking about a difficult event, and (b) acknowledges that the client has both identified and is experiencing strong NA:

> ***Client:*** For me, Christmas is a sad time. My husband died three days after Christmas. So I have a lot of pain there and I don't wanna talk about that because that's done, that was before.
>
> ***Therapist:*** But my sense is that you *are* there right now.
>
> ***Client:*** Yeah.
>
> ***Therapist:*** And you would like it to be done.
>
> ***Client:*** I'd like it to be finished, I'd like to be over with. I'd like that, okay that story's over now and I'm in a new story. But that story is still impacting on me at this point in time.

Similarly, Goldstein and Palmer (1975) described the case of Francis, a person whose "feelings now were centered entirely around the threat (p. 146)" of a divorce from his wife. Francis had experienced a number of difficult life events, including the sudden death of his father when Francis was 12, the unexpected remarriage of his mother when Francis was 16, Francis' marriage to avoid the Vietnam War, and financial and work troubles that resulted in the loss of a $1 million inheritance and the accumulation of $500,000 in debt. His wife had affairs with other men and eventually discovered the extent of Francis' (and thus, the family's) financial difficulties. After his financial troubles surfaced and his wife threatened a divorce (which he did not want), Francis thought about committing suicide—and felt very guilty about such thoughts. Exploring

Francis's guilt about suicidal thoughts is a first step toward helping Francis process his intense affect.

Clients May Talk About Feelings, But Not Experience Them

Difficult to describe precisely, the basic idea is that talking about feelings is not the same as experiencing them. Talking about feelings is not the same state as talking about what one is feeling while experiencing the feeling (i.e, in that moment). Thus, it is difficult to describe how to know whether or not a client is experiencing her or his feelings except to say that such a state is apparent in the client if the therapist is paying close attention.

Some clients use *intellectualizations* throughout the therapy session, which may be a method of avoiding a psychologically painful topic. Particularly with intelligent, verbal clients (and therapists), the dialog can turn to talking about feelings and intellectualizing the material. The following example is from Viney (1993, p. 124):

> ***Therapist:*** Didn't we just establish that you are not offensive to everyone else, only some people?
>
> ***Client:*** It takes a little while to get through my mind because, even though I can accept it emotionally, the wounds are causing me to say, "Hey, you're not, you know." The emotions are arguing back with me.
>
> ***Therapist:*** And that's really why you keep your covered wagon covers down.
>
> ***Client:*** Ooh, yes, I mean, I allow my mental washing to be aired.
>
> ***Therapist:*** What you are really thinking behind those canvasses is, you know, if people really knew me, then they wouldn't want to be close to me.

The therapist may have been more effective by being experience-based and immediate, by focusing on what is happening in the here and now:

> ***Therapist:*** Didn't we just establish that you are not offensive to everyone else, only some people?
>
> ***Client:*** It takes a little while to get through my mind because, even though I can accept it emotionally, the wounds are causing me to say, "Hey, you're not, you know." The emotions are arguing back with me.

Therapist: Let me ask you this: Are you offensive to me, right at this moment?

Client: Well . . . I don't think so.

Therapist: So you're not offensive to everyone.

Client: It's true, with you.

For this client, being "offensive" may be a way of being safe interpersonally. That is, the client may be defensive, afraid of feeling open and vulnerable to others who have the potential to criticize her. So the therapist's intervention—pointing out to the client that she is not offensive to the therapist, in the here and now of the therapeutic situation—is a way of starting an exploration of this issue. Ideally, the therapeutic dialog would move toward processing the client's felt experience of being hurt, shamed, or embarrassed when others have criticized her in the past. In group therapy, the work might also involve asking other group members for feedback about this client's "offensiveness" and the specifics of how others perceive her beyond this narrow label.

While some clients may be aware of their feelings but have difficulty experiencing or expressing them, other individuals may deny or repress feelings. Shedler, Mayman, and Manis (1993) conducted research that suggests that a group of individuals exists that they labeled as *defensive deniers* of psychological distress. Shedler et al. instructed research participants to complete the Beck Depression Inventory, the Eysenck Neuroticism scale, and the Early Memory Test (EMT). The EMT requested accounts of subjects' earliest childhood memories as well as their impressions of themselves, other people, and the mood in the memory. An experienced clinician then evaluated the assessment information to determine each subject's mental health or distress. Finally, participants were exposed to laboratory stressors and experimenters recorded their changes in heart rate and blood pressure. While some participants reported themselves as distressed on the self-reports scales and were also rated as distressed by the clinician, another group reported positive mental health but were rated as distressed by the clinician. This second group of defensive deniers did demonstrate greater reactivity on the physiological measures, suggesting that while these individuals were unaware of their distress, they were more autonomically reactive.

Interrupt Rumination and Avoidance

Individuals who have experienced stressful and traumatic events may employ *self-defensive strategies* in an effort to cope with intrusive memories and their associated intense NA. That is, individuals may be able to recall and describe these events, but the associated psychological distress may motivate them to avoid doing so. The intense distress may reflect NA states such as shame, guilt, anger, anxiety, and depression. With these individuals, therapists face the difficult task of helping clients share their story in a deep enough manner so as to be resolved in some fashion.

Campbell-Sills and Barlow (2007) noted that *suppression* refers to efforts to hide one's feelings from oneself and or others. Other maladaptive methods individuals employ in an attempt to regulate emotion include situational avoidance and social withdrawal, changing situations to alter their impact, use of safety signals (e.g., lucky objects), attention-shifting strategies, rationalization, and substance use. Campbell-Sills and Barlow (2007) indicated research finds that thought suppression typically leads to an increase in unwanted thoughts (i.e., a *rebound effect*). *Avoidance behaviors* maintain anxiety by keeping the individual from exposure and eventual habituation to what currently may be safe situations, or difficult situations that the individual could learn to manage. A person badly frightened by an encounter with a snake in the wild, for example, may avoid the outdoors despite the fact that snake encounters are typically rare. In general, avoidance is a common, but difficult to change, obstacle to progress in therapy.

Therapist: I understand you've been absent from school for two weeks.

Client: People scare me. I get scared when I'm away from home.

Therapist: All people?

Client: No . . . mostly just other kids at school, other guys.

Therapist: So all guys at your school scare you.

Client: The kids who hit me or say they're going to hit me.

Therapist: So you have a good reason why you don't want to go to school.

Client: Yeah. I think about it all the time.

Therapist: What do you think about?

Client: I just think about someone punching me in the hall, or knocking me down in the restroom. I sit in class and can't concentrate because I know that something is going to happen when class is over.

Campbell-Sills and Barlow (2007) maintain that avoidance behaviors are (a) most prevalent in individuals with panic and phobic problems who seek to avoid the experience of fear and (b) associated with increases in NA such as frustration and depression, as individuals lose the positive experiences of their social relationships and other associated activities. In addition, research on autobiographical memories differs regarding the extent to which individuals who have experienced stressful and traumatic events can voluntarily recall the difficult event. Discussing current research on intrusive memories, Berntsen (2010, p. 141) wrote:

> Any distinctive and highly emotional event will be extraordinarily well encoded and consolidated in memory. This will enhance its accessibility relative to other memories and thus increase the likelihood that it comes to mind involuntarily, as well as increase the ease with which it is remembered voluntarily.

Similarly, Kensinger (2007) reviewed evidence indicating that NA enhances subjective vividness of memory and the likelihood of remembering some (but not all) event details.

Individuals dealing with difficult situations may *ruminate* about the situation or related incidents. Ruminations are thoughts that are automatic, intrusive, and distressing (Tedeschi & Calhoun, 2004) and "a class of conscious thoughts that revolve around a common instrumental theme and that recur in the absence of immediate environmental demands requiring the thoughts" (Martin & Tesser, 1996, p. 7).

> ***Therapist:*** So you have a good reason why you don't want to go to school.
>
> ***Client:*** Yeah.
>
> ***Therapist:*** You look worried even while you talk about it.
>
> ***Client:*** Yeah ... it's all I think about at home. What will happen at school.
>
> ***Therapist:*** So staying home keeps you away from the bullies, but it doesn't keep you from worrying about them.

Nolen-Hoeksema (1996, pp. 136–137) maintained that "the key feature of rumination is repetition of a theme in thoughts, without progression toward choice of a solution and a commitment to that solution." Rumination may be considered cognitive problem-solving efforts that an individual cannot easily stop. Research has linked rumination with the duration and onset of depression as well as with impaired social problem solving (Watkins & Moulds, 2005). Watkins and Moulds' (2005) study recommended that rumination be decreased by a combination of (a) focusing attention on the experience of feelings like depression or anxiety and (b) encouraging abstract thinking about the causes and consequences of those feelings. In other words, the client must actively work through the upsetting NA and make sense of it, solve the problem, or come to a resolution (Pennebaker, Zech, & Rimé, 2001).

Explore the Role of Illusions in the Client's Narratives

People can be powerfully motivated by narrative themes that may appear to others as illusory. As children, for example, we may be inspired by the ideals of Cinderella or professional athletes. As Parker (2010, p. 55) wrote about an adult male who appeared motivated by heroic stories of his youth, "To remain attached to the stories that fill [children's] dreams is not peculiar or immature; it's a way to get things done" (p. 55). Similarly, people can be motivated by the dreams and *illusions* of others.

Dreams and illusions may also form an important component in client issues. The categorization of a narrative as illusory depends upon the perception that a person is ignoring some environmental data for feedback. High school or college athletes, for example, may decline career counseling because they believe they will become professional athletes, even though it is highly unlikely that they will do so. These student athletes may have considerable difficulty exploring more realistic but satisfying vocational alternatives. The therapist's task when faced with such narratives is to explore the illusion, its motivation, and the potential consequences for ignoring realistic environmental information.

Bill, for example, is a married, wealthy 58-year-old owner of a large construction company, with offices in major cities. Bill has developed a relationship with Meghan, a 25-year-old employee of his company, who works in a branch office about two hours away from Bill's headquarters. During a typical week they call or text multiple times to tell each other "I love you"; Bill regularly makes expensive purchases for Meghan and takes her out for expensive dinners; Meghan also expects Bill to take care of many problems in her life (e.g., parking tickets, disputes with her neighbors). Although Bill is married, with several young children, his wife knows of this relationship and tolerates it. Bill's presenting problem in therapy is not the affair per se, but Meghan's behavior toward him. Bill becomes distraught when he does not hear from Meghan; she temporarily cuts off contact, for example, when he is unable to solve one of her problems to her satisfaction. In Bill's eyes, Meghan is a source of social esteem, a surrogate trophy wife. He believes that others view him more positively when he is seen in public with Meghan and he feels better about himself when the relationship is going well. Hence, Meghan's manipulative behaviors toward Bill cause him significant distress.

What should the therapist do with such illusions? Most therapists would see the Bill/Meghan relationship as ultimately doomed, although few would outright confront Bill, at least early in therapy. Some might attempt to steer Bill toward a more realistic appraisal (and, eventual ending) of the ultimately unfulfilling nature of his relationship with Meghan. But Bill has a history of seeking out relationships with younger women, and ending the relationship with Meghan is likely to be only a temporary break before he begins with a new, younger woman.

One issue is whether Bill's relationship with his wife (whom he describes as a "great mother," but unattractive physically) can be restored or at least improved. In contrast, he feels energized and happy when the relationship with Meghan is going well; his expectations for the future are upbeat. But he is also vaguely aware that because he spends so much energy on Meghan, he is missing out on relationships with his children.

> ***Bill:*** I care about Meghan a lot, and she really needs a friend. I feel really good when I can help her out and she's grateful.
>
> ***Therapist:*** You work very hard for her.
>
> ***Bill:*** Yes ... but I often feel like I'm on a roller coaster. Half the time she's angry with me because I can't fix some problem or I've disappointed her somehow.
>
> ***Therapist:*** Tell me about the roller coaster.
>
> ***Bill:*** We just go up and down. At least my mood does; I'm happy when I talk with her and worried when I don't hear from her or she doesn't return my calls.
>
> ***Therapist:*** As you speak, you look and sound tired.
>
> ***Bill:*** ... I am ...
>
> ***Therapist:*** As you've described it, this pattern keeps repeating. You do something for her. She's happy or unhappy with what you've done, and then you feel happy or anxious. It's starting to wear you out.
>
> ***Bill:*** ... yes.

Therapist: And when you come home after work and your children want to spend time with you . . .

Bill: I just don't have much energy or interest.

In this instance the therapist helped Bill become explicitly aware of his ambivalence about the relationship with Meghan. The affair brings with it real costs and modest benefits, which Bill has started to explore. Exploring Bill's feelings about these and related issues would seem a natural progression in his therapy.

For some clients, a loss of (what others perceive as) dreams and illusions may be experienced as a loss of meaning. In this vein, Breitbart & Heller (2003) have drawn on the work of Frankl (2000) to study hopelessness, depression, and loss of meaning in terminally ill patients. More specifically, Breitbart and Heller described intervening with end-of-life despair through group psychotherapy and psychoeducation. The goal is to help "patients to identify multiple sources of meaning that still existed in their lives, to teach them a fluid and flexible way to think about those sources of meaning" (Breitbart & Heller, 2003, p. 4). While some may see the pursuit of meaning in persons near death as illusory, the search for and creation of meaning in such individuals may be a valuable way to end their life.

For many clients, the conflict between dreams and eventual experience can be difficult to reconcile. Goodell (2011) wrote an account of her time as a marine in a mortuary unit. She was one of several soldiers who processed the dead bodies of Marines killed in Iraq in preparation for shipment back to the US.

> I believe that every Marine thinks that they are going to die, that it will be a heroic death, one that saves the lives of others. That, however, is a glorified notion, an abstract idea, a vague picture in the mind, a blurry image from a half-remembered movie. We want to save lives, but we haven't grasped what that will entail, and we don't want to grasp it because it may keep us from doing what we will have to do. Knowing exactly what our dream involves will make doing it even harder. (Goodell, 2011, p. 60)

After her tour in Iraq concluded, Goodell (2011, p. 131) wrote about a disappointing meeting with a counselor:

> He didn't tell us that whole spheres of our lives and basic aspects of our selves were gone. Obliterated. That friends and family members and spouses, good memories, sleep, fun, food, and clarity would all have to be shaded black. He didn't tell us that for several of us, our former lives would be shaded black. The

counselor didn't say for a couple of us, hope would be shaded black.

Interrupt Repeated Sequences of Dysfunctional Affect/Cognition/Behaviors

Recall from Chapter 1 that researchers characterize emotions as either universal basic emotions (BEs), such as PA and NA, or emotional schemas (ESs), in which individuals think idiosyncratically about their emotions as well as the situations that elicited those emotions (Izard, 2007). One reason why clients may have difficulty accessing and sharing their feelings is that the feelings are stuck in ESs. Izard (2007) suggested that in comparison to BEs, ESs are greater in frequency and longer in duration. They can be complex concatenations of feelings and thoughts that may be difficult to recognize and untangle.

Teyber and McClure (2011) offered a similar idea when they suggested that many clients present with *constellations of feelings*. These are basic emotions that are linked and typically occur in a predictable sequence. Teyber and McClure suggested that common groupings are anger–sadness–shame and sadness–anger–guilt. One of these feelings is likely to be the trigger for the sequence, and Teyber and McClure recommend that once the therapist has identified that primary emotion, the therapeutic focus should begin there. Recall this example from Chapter 2:

> ***Client:*** I guess I've let my world collapse. People at work have begun complaining about me. And I've been like a zombie most of the time.
>
> ***Therapist:*** Your world has collapsed?
>
> ***Client:*** I've been drinking again and missing a lot of work. My boss wants to know why I've missed the last two staff meetings.
>
> ***Therapist:*** Ok, you've been sober for two years. When did you start to drink again?
>
> ***Client:*** Management started to talk about layoffs when sales dropped last quarter. I was worried about what I would do if I got laid off—who would hire a 55-year-old man in this economy?
>
> ***Therapist:*** So you were anxious about losing your job.
>
> ***Client:*** Yes, and I was home sick one day, and I thought, what harm would one drink do? That was about two weeks ago, and between the stress and drinking, I've been a mess.

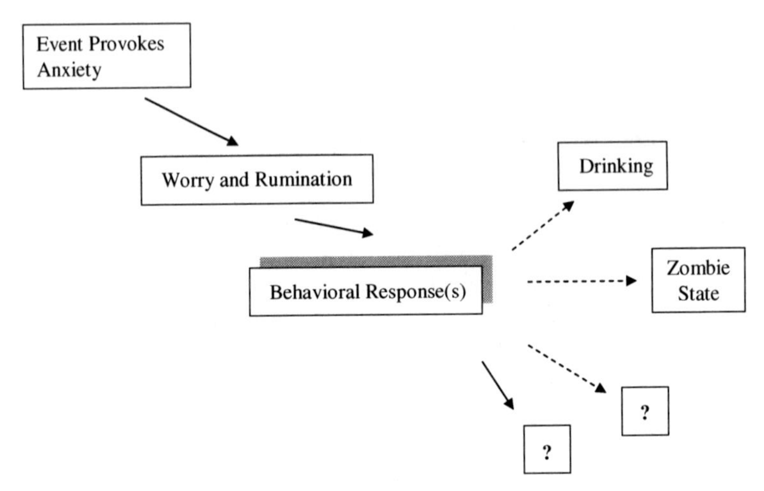

FIGURE 5.1 *Affective–cognition–behavioral linkages for World Collapses Zombie.*
Note: *Following an event that the client interprets as anxiety-producing, he begins to ruminate about the event and its implications. Through drinking and feeling like a "zombie," he behaves in a manner designed to decrease the anxiety and the accompanying rumination.*

When the therapist senses that relatively complex linkages are present, it may be useful to represent the reports in a diagram and modify it over time as more observations occur (Meier, 2003). These are working hypotheses whose explicit representation in a graph or drawing may make it easier for the therapist to remember and think about (Teyber & McClure, 2011). Figure 5.1 shows one possible depiction for the client in the example above.

One question that the therapist and client could explore is what other behavioral responses could be generated that could help the client cope with the initial anxiety in a more healthy and productive manner. In other words, what behaviors, thoughts, or feelings (even in tiny amounts) could be substituted for any of the steps in this sequence?

THERAPIST ISSUES

Therapy can be well described as a learned *craft*, which implies that the skilled clinician has a focus and a discipline learned through years of training and supervision. Consequently, therapy skills include knowing what *not* to do as well as what to do. The skills set discussed in this half of the chapter focuses on the clinician's management of affect, thoughts, and behavior in clients' narratives. Equally important to therapeutic progress is the clinician's self-regulation. Some therapists, particularly those without regular supervision, can lose their discipline and spend too much time in therapy telling personal narratives instead of listening to their clients. Therapists' clinical narratives may also blind them to important aspects of their clients. And like their clients, therapists' own feelings may hinder the therapeutic process.

Do Not Get in the Way of the Client's Storytelling

Most clients are willing to share with the therapist at least some important themes and details. One of the therapist's first tasks, consequently, is not to get in the way of their client's narration (McLeod, 1997). Therapists can obstruct clients any number of ways, including overloading clients with information, speaking too much, and self-disclosing too much.

> ***Client:*** My dad got angry at me, so I went to the store and got something to eat.
>
> ***Therapist:*** So your father lost his temper again, and as usual, you got a stomachache when you started to feel anxious about your dad's yelling. I wonder if you were eating as a way to manage your anxiety or whether you just needed to get out of the house? Is there something else you can do to change that the next time your dad becomes angry?

In this example, nothing the therapist said is wrong or misleading—it's just too much information at once. One of these three sentences would have been sufficient.

With some exceptions (e.g., when summarizing), therapists talk less than their clients, often communicating in one or two sentences (Meier & Davis, 2011). Beginning therapists typically have difficulty being brief, as may experienced clinicians who are stressed or have lost some of their professional discipline over the years.

In ordinary conversations with two people, a frequently employed norm is that both parties talk in roughly equal amounts (Grice, 1991). Counseling and psychotherapeutic conversations, however, differ with their focus on therapeutic goals of the client. From a narrative and language perspective, many of the techniques taught to beginning therapists, such as minimal encouragers, speaking briefly, reflection of feelings and content, use of open-ended questions, and allowing silence, keep the therapist from interfering with the client's storytelling (Meier & Davis, 2011). Again, recall this example:

> ***Client:*** I guess I've let my world collapse. People at work have begun complaining about me. And I've been like a zombie most of the time.

Therapist: Uh-huh . . . (nodding)

Client: I've been drinking again and missing a lot of work. My boss wants to know why I've missed the last two staff meetings.

Therapist: Ok . . . (silence, but therapist is clearly listening to the client)

Client: Management started to talk about layoffs when sales dropped last year. I was worried about what I would do if I got laid off—who would hire a 55-year-old man in this economy?

Therapist: You were worried about losing your job.

Client: Yes, and I was home sick one day, and I thought, what harm would one drink do? That was about two weeks ago, and between the stress and drinking, I've been a mess.

One clear indicator that a therapist has mastered basic listening skills is when she or he can (appropriately) proceed through an entire session by relying on minimal encouragers and brief statements. In contrast, a therapist might speak more when providing an intervention or conducting an intake interview.

Ordinary and therapeutic conversations can also be distinguished by the amount of silence. During silent moments, clients may be processing internal experiences and affect. Levitt (2002) proposed that during silent periods, clients are internally processing in one of three different ways: (a) *emotional*, where clients attend to strong feelings that arose during the therapeutic conversation, (b) *expressive*, where clients are trying to produce labels or language to describe what they were experiencing, or (c) *reflective*, where clients seek meaning or make connections of what they were experiencing. Producing such silent periods, according to Levitt and Rennie (2004, p. 303), should be a major goal of therapy "because they lead to a narrative that reflects a deepened awareness of self." Because silence can feel awkward, it requires discipline and practice for therapists-in-training to be comfortable with periods of silence while clients process internally.

Do Not Assume You Understand the Meaning of What Clients Say

The richness of human language means that verbal and nonverbal communications generally have the potential for ambiguity and multiple meanings. This principle is similar to the idea proposed by Meier and Davis (2011): *Do not assume that you know clients' feelings, thoughts, and behaviors.* In ordinary conservation, we generally assume that we understand what others are saying to us, that is, both speaker and listener typically assume that the speaker is attempting to communicate in a nonambiguous manner (Grice, 1991). Therapists who learn listening skills often quickly discover the fallacy of this assumption (Meier & Davis, 2011).

> ***Client:*** So I just left after we started to argue.
>
> ***Therapist:*** You were very angry.
>
> ***Client:*** No, I had to leave for work in 10 minutes, and I knew we'd never finish the argument in that time.

One of the reasons therapists may misunderstand client communication is *countertransference*, the therapist's reactions and feelings to the client's communications. Countertransference has the potential to influence the therapist's perception of the client's communication as well as how the therapist subsequently responds to the client. To the extent that the therapist has strong feelings and unresolved issues about topics the client is discussing, or aspects of the interaction and relationship with the client, the possibility for therapist misinterpretation and miscommunication is enhanced.

The same idea applies to client nonverbal communication. While a universal set of facial expressions exists (Matsumoto, 2001), in general, therapists should check out the meaning of any particular client nonverbal expression. Therapists trust nonverbal communication as a source of information since it is more difficult to censor than verbal statements.

> ***Therapist:*** I've noticed that as the session has gone on you've folded your arms together and that you're rubbing your hands together. I'm wondering if this topic has made you feel a bit vulnerable?
>
> ***Client:*** Not really. It's cold in your office and I forgot to bring a sweater!

Because of the possibility of misunderstanding, good therapists typically listen with a sense of tentativeness and a willingness to explore the meaning of client statements to clarify meaning. The typical form for this tentativeness is for the therapist to reflect feeling or content and follow up with a clarifying question (Meier & Davis, 2011):

> ***Therapist:*** You seem sad as you speak of your father. Is that how you feel?

Client: No, I didn't feel sad as much as I felt angry about getting into another argument.

Learn to Tolerate Clients' Discomfort

Experienced therapists understand that some interactions with clients will make the therapist uncomfortable. Therapists may inadvertently hinder client progress, for example, by avoiding clients' strong feelings (Teyber & McClure, 2011). Many therapists perceive themselves as nice people who are natural helpers. Therapists typically do not see themselves as the cause of client pain, but as healers and doctors who help to decrease pain. Therapists-in-training can become uncomfortable when they perceive themselves as the source of that pain. One of the important tasks in supervision is to monitor how students feel about and react to their clients' presentation, particularly the client's NA.

That therapists may avoid client feelings will be evident to anyone who has been a graduate student in a mental health field or trained such students. One student in a doctoral program, for example, burst into laughter upon hearing a client express strong affect. Therapists may have strong reactions, for example, when clients (a) discuss problems similar to those of the therapist, (b) behave in a hostile or aggressive manner toward the therapist, or (c) are dealing with situations (e.g., trauma) or strong emotions (e.g., homicidal feelings) for which the therapist has had little personal or professional experience (Teyber & McClure, 2011).

One situation that can be vexing for both therapists-in-training and experienced therapists is the aggressive client who attacks the therapist. Part of the problem is that in many settings, this type of client is relatively infrequent, and so gaining relevant experience is difficult. Nevertheless, most therapists will need to manage difficult clients who externalize some of their problems onto the therapist. The following example is adapted from a case described by Teyber and McClure (2011). Ann was a chronically depressed and irritable client working with Mary, an intern. Ann was unhappy with Mary because her depression was not improving. She criticized Mary, as she had a history of doing with her husband and other people:

Ann: I keep coming here every week, but you're not doing anything to make me better!

Mary (stunned): Tell me more.

Ann: Sometimes I don't even know where we're going or what we're trying to accomplish here.

> ***Mary:*** Okay . . .
>
> ***Ann:*** Is there someone with more experience than an intern who could help me?
>
> ***Mary:*** I can ask about that, but I think you're getting better. Certainly the last couple of weeks you've been making progress.

Teyber and McClure (2011) reported that Mary's supervisor worked with her to acknowledge Ann's anger and discuss her dissatisfaction. Their summary statement to Ann (Teyber & McClure, 2011, p. 227) follows:

> ***Mary:*** Your depression isn't getting better and it doesn't feel like I'm helping you. I respect your honesty and appreciate how you're bringing this up so directly. Let's talk more about what hasn't felt useful here and see if we can come up with some different ways of working together that might be better. Tell me more about what has been frustrating or disappointing you.

This approach is essentially an invitation to process the client's feelings with the therapist (although the last sentence in the example might suffice for such an invitation). With some planning, another option would be to confront the client by pointing out the client's history of criticizing others and exploring the triggers and consequences for the criticism.

Teyber and McClure (2011) also described a first-year practicum student who was receiving very different instructions from her practicum instructor and onsite supervisor about how to proceed with clients. This situation was intensified by the student's experience as a child when she had to deal with her divorcing parents and frequently felt that she had failed to "please 'both sides'" (Teyber & McClure, 2011, p. 218). This context became an acute problem one day in therapy with Maria, a client who was relating a story of a date rape from 15 years earlier. After hearing this story, the student therapist struggled for a full minute trying to find what she thought were the right words to respond to Maria (Teyber & McClure, 2011, p. 219, transcript slightly edited):

> ***Maria:*** Don't you understand? He hurt me a lot when he did that!
>
> ***Student Therapist:*** Yes. He did hurt you very much—it was frightening and infuriating . . . and I understand why you are angry at me for not responding. I was touched by what you said, but I just couldn't find the right words for a minute.
>
> ***Maria:*** You couldn't?

> ***Student Therapist:*** No, I was trying to so hard, because I felt for you. But I just couldn't find the words I wanted to say, and the harder I searched for them, the worse it got. I'm sorry this happened; it must have been hurtful for you.
>
> ***Maria:*** It's OK . . . This makes me think of my daughter when she was little. If I would take the time to stop and pick her up and really listen to her when she needed me, we could get through her problem pretty quick. My husband called it "collecting her."
>
> ***Student Therapist:*** You're a good mom. I think you're remembering that right now because that's what you needed from me—to be attended to, cared about, collected. You needed me to give you what you have your daughter.
>
> ***Maria:*** Yeah, I think that's just exactly what I needed. (*tearing*) You know, I never dreamed of telling my mother what happened to me—you know, about the date rape. She needed me to be "happy" all the time; she didn't want to hear about problems . . . not even big ones.

By processing what had just happened with Maria in a nondefensive manner, the student therapist helped Maria recall an important event and reconnected with her. Notice that the therapist did not self-disclose her personal or professional issues regarding the cause of the difficulty, but kept the discussion pertinent to Maria and their immediate conversation. Maria also offered a metaphor potentially useful for future use: The idea of "collecting" the client, of taking the time to listen and care about her problems. This might be useful language for assessing whether a therapist (or another person, such as a friend or her husband) was able to be helpful to Maria with a particular problem or during a particular session. It might also be useful to know if "collecting" her helped Maria to move through that problem "pretty quick" or if more time would be helpful.

A final example: A school counselor-in-training reported working with a client who expressed deep sadness when the counselor would direct the client toward the topic of her parent's divorce. The counselor felt like she was "opening a huge wound" and that the counselor was then responsible for the client's feelings. The student counselor also felt that she either needed to fix the feelings when they arose or avoid focusing the client on the feelings altogether. This counselor's supervisor was able to provide a rationale for why the client should work through these feelings rather than avoid them.

As described in Chapter 3, one strategy that may be helpful for therapists in these situations is to remember the principles of *pacing and leading* the client. When a therapist paces a client, the therapist essentially follows along in terms of the content and affective intensity presented by the client. Leading refers to the therapist's introduction of new material or process. When a therapist observes that a client has difficulty handling intense affect and moves away from it, then, it may be useful to pace that client for a while. Each client is likely to have different tolerances for how much NA they may handle, and through the process of pacing and leading the therapist can help make this process manageable.

Be Cautious About Using Affect as a Diagnosis

Labeling an emotion as a diagnosis may be misleading with many clients. Such labeling can become problematic if a client begins to view her- or himself as *depressed* (a characterological trait) rather than a person *with depression* (a situationally induced state). One of the functions of *externalizing* a problem is to give a person more psychological control over the NA or other label they are experiencing. While some clients feel comforted by the reduced uncertainty of a diagnosis, placing the problem within the person, as a stable condition, may complicate therapeutic interventions.

If emotions function as a signal of a person's situation in an environment, then states such as anxiety or depression are not the problem per se but an indicator of a problem. Thus, a person may be anxious because she anticipates losing her job; losing a job, with its desired income and social interactions, is the problem for the person and anxiety a bodily based indicator of the person's appraisal of the problem in context. Similarly, a person may report being depressed over the loss of an important relationship. If the anxious person receives assurance that his job is secure, the anxiety is likely to abate. Likewise, if the depressed person begins a new relationship, the depression will likely decrease. In both cases, the feelings of anxiety and depression are *primary emotional reactions* to the perceived problematic situation.

But psychotherapists also see individuals in which an improvement in the problematic situation does not lead to a significant change in affect. These individuals are reacting to their primary emotion, what might be labeled a *secondary* or *looped emotional reaction* (cf. Teyber & McClure, 2011). The anxious person is so uncomfortable by the experience of anxiety that she attempts to suppress the feeling and thereby extends it over time and across situations. The depressed person is ashamed of being saddened by the relationship loss and now feels anxious whenever he begins a new relationship. As shown in Figure 5.2, the central problem has become the person's feelings about his or her feelings.

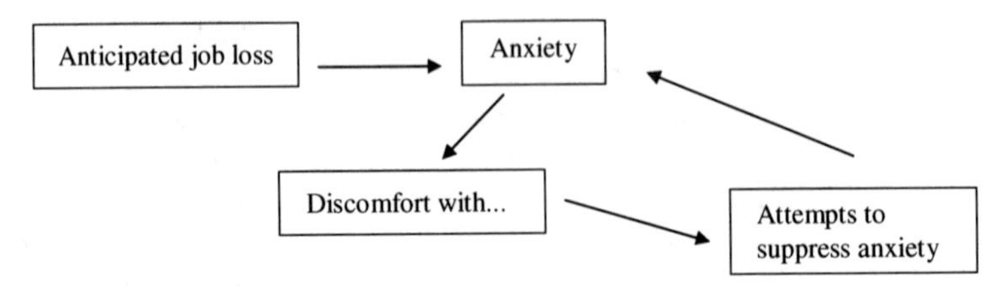

***FIGURE* 5.2** *Primary and secondary emotional reactions.*
Note: *A problematic situation (e.g., anticipated job loss) leads to an emotional reaction (e.g., anxiety). However, the person has a secondary reaction (e.g., discomfort with anxiety) to the primary affect (anxiety) and subsequently attempts to suppress the anxiety. That effort, however, leads to increased and sustained anxiety.*

Panic attacks may be the best clinical example of a secondary emotional reaction that perpetuates an initial emotional reaction (Tull & Roemer, 2007). Many persons with panic attacks appear to have strong reactions to bodily experiences of anxiety or fear. Once they notice they are feeling anxious, this signals the presence of a problem that cascades into increasing arousal and physical symptoms such as shortness of breath and dizziness.

Clinical Narratives Can Become an Expression of Hypothesis Confirmation Bias

Therapists also construct stories about their clients, typically about client problems and the causes of those problems. Therapeutic problems occur when a diagnostic narrative is misleading and yet the therapist continues to hold that narrative. Even when clinical data do not support the diagnosis, therapists may hold to a treatment plan based on that misleading narrative. The 1995 PBS broadcast of an episode of *Frontline* entitled "The Search for Satan," for example, describes two young female patients, Pat and Mary, who were treated by a team of inpatient psychiatrists, psychologists, and social workers (summarized in Meier, 2008b).

Mary sought therapy because she had been experiencing panic attacks, weight loss, and difficulty concentrating. She had recently been attacked in a hallway at the school where she taught and had a history that indicated that she might be vulnerable to depression. Date-raped at age 19, she became pregnant and gave the child up for adoption; her husband was an alcoholic, and after the birth of her son, Mary had a hysterectomy and developed seizures. The seizures and blackouts led her therapist to refer Mary for evaluation of a possible dissociative disorder. Pat sought therapy after being depressed for three years following the difficult birth of one of her two sons. She was referred to the same team of mental health professionals as Mary, who diagnosed both with multiple personality disorder (MPD) and believed they were members of a satanic cult.

Depression appears to be a simpler diagnosis for Mary and Pat than MPD in terms of clinical symptoms, but the clinical treatment team appeared to dismiss any disconfirming evidence. Outside of the mental health professionals' interpretation of their symptoms, no evidence apparently existed that indicated Pat or Mary had participated or been a victim of a satanic cult. Instead, the clinicians appear to be operating on the basis of a *hypothesis confirmation bias* (HCB), where a clinician prematurely decides on a clinical diagnosis hypothesis and then proceeds to ignore any subsequent information that disconfirms that diagnosis hypothesis. One of Pat's sons, for example, related a story of alleged satanic abuse when he described cutting open a person's stomach with a knife and watching the guts pop out. While Pat reported that the story was a fabrication based on a scene in a *Star Wars* movie, one mental health professional insisted it was true (independent of any other corroborating evidence). Even as her treatment continued, Mary's psychological condition worsened over several years. Scheduled to be moved to a nursing home, Mary refused and discontinued treatment; she saw another therapist outside the hospital, discontinued her medications, and physically regained her health. Pat also stopped medications and hypnosis and her symptoms also disappeared.

Noteworthy about both cases is that the clinicians apparently had no systematic method of obtaining clinical data that could provide useful feedback about Mary or Pat's progress. Despite Mary and Pat's continued distress, the clinicians' apparent belief in the validity of their diagnosis meant that they continued treatment that both Pat and Mary eventually reported as ineffectual and harmful.

How can therapists avoid HCB in their narratives about clients? While most therapists are familiar with the concept of tentativeness in terms of how therapists approach clients, therapists should also treat case conceptualizations tentatively as well. Experienced therapists may have a very good idea of how a specific client is likely to make sense of a difficult situation, such as resolving the death of a loved one. For both the client and therapist's sake, however, the therapist would be wise to hold those expectations tentatively. The temptation with the client is to move that person toward the expected resolution prematurely. Anderson and Goolishian (1990, p. 159) discuss tentativeness as a position of "not-knowing": that is, therapy is a process of "moving toward what is *not yet known*." In general, a therapist's best strategy is to *not* assume that they completely understand what is happening with the client. Holding ideas about the client with a sense of tentativeness may help the therapist avoid HCB.

In a high-stakes clinical situation such as with Pat and Mary, a more resource-intensive approach for avoiding HCB involves developing a case conceptualization and gathering clinical data to evaluate the conceptualization (Meier, 2003). Researchers and practitioners in fields such as education and medicine have employed outcome data to improve the results of ongoing interventions (Cross & Angelo, 1988). By providing *feedback* to persons involved in or providing an intervention, the likelihood of client improvement, and avoiding client deterioration, is enhanced. Kluger and DeNisi's (1996) meta-analysis of feedback studies showed that persons receiving feedback on various tasks outperform persons who are not, while Sapyta's (2004) meta-analysis of 30 randomized clinical trials where health professionals received feedback about client health status in the community had better outcomes.

Despite such research, Claiborn and Goodyear (2005, p. 215) noted that "feedback is often not specified as a theory-based component of psychological treatment." Recent psychotherapy research, however, has found benefits for employing structured feedback and clinical support tools as part of the therapeutic process (Clement, 1994, 1999). In *patient-focused research*, clinicians receive direct feedback about a client's progress (Howard et al., 1996). Using the Outcome Questionnaire (OQ-45) as a progress measure, Lambert et al. (2001) examined the effect of providing feedback to therapists working with two types of college counseling clients, those evidencing improvement and those who were not. Using clients' weekly OQ-45 data, therapists received progress reports to learn which clients had an adequate rate of improvement, an inadequate rate of change, or were failing to make any progress. Results indicated a benefit for providing feedback to clinicians: OQ scores at termination were higher for clients who were initially not making progress, but whose therapist was receiving feedback, compared to clients who were not progressing and whose therapist received no feedback. Similarly, Lambert, Harmon, Slade, Whipple, and Hawkins (2005), examining the results of four studies that evaluated the effects of clinical feedback with over 2,500 clients, found that feedback enhanced outcomes for patients with a negative response. Therapists who received progress feedback with clients not making initial improvement saw those clients evidence less deterioration and more improvement over time than clients with therapists not receiving feedback. Therapists given feedback about their clients' lack of improvement tended to keep those clients in treatment for more sessions. Based on these results, Lambert et al. (2005, p. 171) recommended "widespread application of feedback systems in routine care."

While these studies focus on providing feedback to the therapist, it may also be useful to share data-based feedback with clients. A number of researchers and clinicians have described methods of presenting data via understandable graphics to help clients understand change on outcome measures over time. For more information, readers should consult Ahmed and Boisvert (2003), Corcoran and Gingerich (1994), Gottman and Leiblum (1974), and Meier (2003).

SUMMARY AND IMPLICATIONS

This chapter described and presented potential solutions to a range of narrative-related obstacles introduced by clients and therapists. For clients, a primary barrier to therapeutic progress is reluctance to explore, experience, or express strong NA such as sadness and shame. Rumination and avoidance behaviors, for example, can result from clients' inability to stay with and process intense NA. Therapists, including therapists-in-training, may also have difficulty staying with clients who possess and express strong NA. Such difficulties may be evident when therapists talk too much or give advice. Therapists can also mistakenly presume to understand clients' statements and language, and they can also misapply clinical narratives that do not usefully fit a client.

These obstacles influence whether and how much clients can progress in therapy. The next chapter will describe several methods for tracking progress using narrative- and language-related constructs.

Six

Assessment

From a narrative perspective, what constructs would suggest that a client has changed? This chapter describes existing as well as innovative methods for providing progress and outcome data related to narrative constructs. While only a relatively brief survey of possibilities, the measures described in this chapter offer the clinician and researcher good options for assessing the affect, cognitions, and behaviors most relevant to client narratives. The chapter does not delve deeply into technical details about measurement and assessment, but provides an overview of assessment challenges along with descriptions of several practical methods. Readers who have not completed a course in psychological testing are cautioned about the use of the methods described here unless they are working with appropriate supervision.

The methods in this chapter depend upon two different types of methodology technology: *Quantitative data* produced by *psychological tests* and *qualitative data* present in clinical *progress notes*. Historically, tests have been developed for selection decisions, that is, to classify or make decisions about large groups of individuals (Haywood, Brown, & Wingenfeld, 1990). Tests like the SAT or GRE, for example, are intended to help decide whom to admit to college or graduate programs. Use of the qualitative data found in progress notes, on the other hand, is a type of *assessment*, which refers to a human judge's use of data from sources such as interviews or observations. *Assessment* is a broader term than *psychological test* and includes any measurement method that involves human judgment; this includes interpretation of clinical progress notes to determine the degree and type of client progress.

WHY DOES CLINICAL ASSESSMENT MATTER?

Assessment provides feedback. Most importantly, clinical assessment lets us know when we make mistakes and how to identify those mistakes in the therapeutic process. Moreover, research indicates that mistakes do

Note: Portions of this chapter are based on Meier (2008b).

occur in clinical practice: Estimates place the rate of *treatment failure* between 10% and 50% of all clients (Kendall, Kipnis, & Otto-Salaj, 1992; Persons & Mikami, 2002). These clients fail to make progress or worsen over the course of therapy.

As described in Chapter 5, an episode of *Frontline* entitled "The Search for Satan" described two young women, Pat and Mary, who were treated by a team of hospital-based mental health professionals. After several years of treatment where they showed no improvement or worsened, both Mary and Pat stopped therapy on their own. The consequences of these treatment failures were serious. For example, Mary's husband filed for divorce, the state of Illinois listed her as a child abuser, and her son did not wish to see her. Mary's insurer paid about $2.5 million for her treatment and Pat's insurer paid $3 million dollars for treatment of her and her sons.

Although the *Frontline* episode provided relatively little information regarding the therapists' decision-making for these individuals, it appeared that the therapists had few methods for testing the belief that satanic ritual abuse, or some alternative process, was the cause of Mary's or Pat's problems. Therapists also apparently had few methods for obtaining feedback about progress outside of their clinical judgment, and they appeared to dismiss feedback from other professionals (e.g., nurses) about their lack of effectiveness. Particularly in cases where clients worsen, or fail to make progress over extended periods, it is important to obtain assessment data to inform decisions about therapeutic interventions and potential adjustments. But this can be more difficult than most therapists realize.

MEASUREMENT CHALLENGES IN CLINICAL PROGRESS AND OUTCOME ASSESSMENT

For all the expertise that mental health providers have for creating and delivering interventions, a major weakness of the field is the lack of instruments purposely designed for assessing progress and outcome in psychotherapy (Meier, 2008b). For both practice and research, this is a major sticking point for progress in the field.

All scientific domains appear to grapple with measurement problems as part of their historical development. As noted in Chapter 1, Tryon (1991, p. 1) observed that "the history of science is largely coextensive with the history of measurement," while Cone (1988, p. 42) wrote that "it is certainly beyond argument that the building of all science rests on a foundation of accurate measurement." New measurement techniques drive scientific development (Cone & Foster, 1991; Forbes & Dijksterhuis, 1963). For example, refinement of methods of measuring adenine and thymine along with advancements in X-ray technology made possible Watson and Crick's discovery of the structure of DNA (Meehl, 1991). Scientific progress is not only dependent upon measurement advances, but new techniques allow refined tests between rival theories and hypotheses (cf. Ellis, 1967). Innovation in measurement theory and techniques appears important for progress in any science (Judson, 1980; Kuhn, 1970); measurement devices provide new data for ideas, extend human senses, and correct for limitations of the senses (Tryon, 1991).

Most contemporary psychological tests have been developed with test construction methodologies that identify items reflective of psychological *traits*, constructs that evidence stability over time and across situations (Meier, 1994, 2008b). In contrast, with most measures employed to measure progress and outcome, therapists assess psychological *states*, constructs that can change over time and situations. The misapplication of traditional psychological tests for use in counseling and psychotherapy means that unexpected or surprising results are likely to be frequent occurrences in clinical research. The degree of apparent change resulting from a psychotherapeutic intervention, for example, can be influenced by both *assessment method* and the specific *psychological test* chosen (Lambert, 1994). Lambert (1994, p. 85) concluded:

> There are reliable differences in the sensitivity of instruments to change ... Meta-analytic results suggest that the most popular dependent measures used to assess depression following treatment provide reliably different pictures of change.

Lambert, Hatch, Kingston, and Edwards (1986) compared the Zung, Beck, and Hamilton depression scales as outcome measures of mental health interventions. They found "that rating devices can by themselves produce differences larger than those ordinarily attributed to treatments" (Lambert et al., 1986, p. 58). The self-report Beck Depression Inventory (BDI), one of the most frequently used outcome measures in both research and practice, contains multiple-choice items assessing different aspects of depression (Beck & Steer, 1987); a second version of the BDI, the Beck Depression Inventory II (BDI II) (Beck, Steer, & Brown, 1996), conforms to diagnostic criteria listed in the *Diagnostic and Statistical Manual of Mental Disorders*, 4th edition (*DSM-IV*) (Nezu, Ronan, Meadows, & McClure, 2000). BDI items assess cognitions, somatic responses, and affect related to depression, including mood, guilt feelings, suicidal wishes, irritability, sleep disturbance, and appetite changes. Research suggests that the BDI can function as a reliable and valid measure for the purpose of diagnosing and screening for depression (Segal, Williams, & Teasdale, 2002). Research results, however, have raised questions about the validity of the BDI when the intended purpose is to measure change. Over 50% of individuals classified as depressed by the BDI change depression categories when retested, even when the retesting period consisted of only a few hours or days (Kendall, Hollon, Beck, Hammen, & Ingram, 1987). BDI scores have also exhibited sudden, unexplained increases and decreases between psychotherapy sessions (Kelly, Roberts, & Ciesla, 2005). These results raise questions, when assessing progress and outcome, about the extent to which change on scores on this instrument can be attributed to psychotherapy versus other influences.

ASSESSMENT METHODS

Story Characteristics

Story characteristics refer to the broad range of concepts proposed to describe and evaluate the types, structures, purposes, and forms of client narratives. Table 6.1 presents a sample of characteristics proposed for measurement purposes in the narrative therapies literature. Hardtke and Angus (2004), for example, distinguished between *micronarratives*, stories

TABLE 6.1 Examples of Assessment Targets Suggested by Narrative Therapies

Author (Year)	*Concept*	*Relevance to assessment*
Angus & McLeod (2004)	Chronicles/ reports	Stories with no sense of drama or purpose
Angus & McLeod (2004)	Cultural narratives	Stories of the good life
Dimaggio & Semerari (2004)	Diagnostic stories	Tone or style of story indicates *DSM* diagnosis (e.g., lack of positive valence indicates depression)
Greenberg & Angus (2004)	Affect	Affect shapes many aspects of stories
Hardtke & Angus (2004)	Micronarratives	Stories told in the therapy hour
	Macronarratives	A life story
Singer & Blagov (2004)	Integrative statements	Reports of lessons learned from life experiences
Singer & Blagov (2004)	Self-defining memories	The main elements of personality and identity, including personal goals; can possess affective intensity and vividness

Note: Adapted from Meier (2008b).

told in the therapy hour, and *macronarratives*, the client's life story. Angus and McLeod (2004) described *chronicles* or *reports* (i.e., stories with no sense of drama or purpose) and *cultural narratives* (stories of the good life). Life stories may include components that are incompatible with each other, indicating the presence of *multiple, fragmented identities* (Angus & McLeod, 2004).

As noted in Chapter 3, client stories usually do not encompass all of a person's life experiences, and some of the *excluded experiences* may be important to a healthy sense of self. Some types of dysfunction may be evident by the absence of key story elements (Anderson, 2004), while other important life experiences may contradict the dominant story. For example, a therapist-in-training who sees himself as a natural helper may find it difficult to accept feedback from a supervisor who tells him that he has poor listening skills. One method for ascertaining what has been excluded or distorted in client narratives is to evaluate the story's coherence or organization (Angus & McLeod, 2004; McAdams, 1996). Table 6.2 presents a list of potential criteria (Angus & McLeod, 2004) that imply that progress in therapy is marked by the development of well-formed narratives about the client's problematic situation(s).

Research indicates that the narratives of clients who are improving should be marked by a decrease in negative affect (NA), an increase in positive affect (PA), and an increase in the number and plausibility of explanations for the motivation of major characters (Pennebaker et al., 2003). Smyth (1998, p. 174) concluded that "written emotional expression leads to the transduction of the traumatic experience into a linguistic structure that promotes assimilation and understanding of the event, and reduces negative affect associated with thoughts of the event." In other words, clients become deconditioned to the trauma and make sense of the experience. Similarly, Pennebaker (Pennebaker, 1993; Pennebaker, Mayne, & Francis, 1997) concluded that narratives that became more focused and coherent over writing sessions were associated with health improvements; verbalizing affective experiences into an organized linguistic form would seem to be a key component (Pennebaker et al., 1997).

Angus and McLeod (2004) are among those who have proposed that story characteristics can be linked to client diagnosis and psychopathology. The stories of borderlines are marked by the presence of overwhelming emotion; similarly, Dimaggio and Semerari (2004, p. 267) described borderlines as telling stories "loaded with extreme judgments—all good or all bad—toward the self and significant others." Depressed individuals have difficulty identifying specific story elements when asked to narrate positive experiences (Anderson, 2004). Autistic individuals tend to be very precise in describing objects and characters but fail to include agency and emotion (Angus & McLeod, 2004, p. 323). Research conducted by cognitive behavioral clinicians has found that the memories of trauma victims are

TABLE 6.2 A Sample of Criteria for Well-Formed Narratives From Angus & McLeod (2004)

Criteria for good form	*If not?*
Internally consistent	Events in the story appear implausible or seem to "come out of nowhere"
Makes sense to others	Listener may perceive the story as "weird"
Richness of themes	Listener may have difficulty sustaining attention to story as it is told; poor content regarding descriptions of characters and events
Organization	Disorganized, difficult to follow
Story has a beginning, middle, and end	Missing one of these components, or one of the components insubstantial (e.g., lacks a meaningful ending) or ill-fitting
Character(s)'s motivation apparent	Lack of empathy or insight into others; interpersonal skills
Character(s)'s affect apparent	Lack of insight into motivation, context
Credible elements	Obvious falsehoods present; elements so unfamiliar to audience that story is not credible; no obstacles present
Positive/negative dimension	Depressed individuals may have difficulty identifying positive aspects of experiences
Generality/specificity dimension	Stories that are too general may be indicative of working memory problems

disorganized and fragmented (Amir, Stafford, Freshman, & Foa, 1998); treatment with prolonged exposure therapy was associated with increased organization in the narrative around trauma (Foa, Molnar, & Cashman, 1995). Smyth's (1998) review also found evidence for associations between memory disorganization and trauma (e.g., Foa & Kozak, 1986; Foa & Riggs, 1993). Reflecting the organization concept proposed by McAdams (1996), traumatic memories appear to be disorganized and treatments such as exposure therapy and writing procedures appear to reduce that disorganization (Pennebaker, 1993).

Self-Descriptions

Some story characteristics focus specifically on self-descriptions (Hardtke & Angus, 2004). *Self-efficacy*, one's sense of personal competence for specific tasks, has been previously discussed as a potentially key element of client stories. Singer and Blagov (2004) focused on what they term *self-defining memories*, which include the main elements of personality and identity, including personal goals (cf. Hardtke & Angus, 2004, regarding self-image). Self-defining memories of therapeutic interest are those that possess affective intensity and vividness and relate to an important unresolved concern. They can be considered critical incidents that occur within and outside therapy sessions that are remembered by the client for their special significance about the client. Singer and Blagov (2004, p. 239) suggested that "images from these memories serve as metaphoric touchstones in the therapeutic dialogue," helping the client to draw lessons from different, linked experiences.

Self-descriptions are also the focus of the Narrative Assessment Interview (NAI), a brief semi-structured interview administered at the start of therapy and at follow-up periods (Hardtke & Angus, 2004). Three questions are administered in the interview: (a) How would you describe yourself? (b) How would someone who knows you really well describe you? (c) If you could change something about who you are, what would you change? The research then conducts a content analysis of the person's answers to each question in order to produce a summary sheet of key information. Finally, at the end of therapy, the client reviews this summary sheet and reflects on this information.

Assessing Affect

Negative Affect

As described in Chapter 2, descriptions of client problems typically include NA. Viney (1993) reported the case of June, a 55-year-old woman who came to a university clinic with difficulties with her marriage and family. Describing her marriage as "30 years of frustration and hell" (Viney, 1993, p. 114), June herself was:

> . . . ridden with emotions such as frustration, anger, suspicion, as well as depression. Her depressive feelings were linked to feelings of rejection and loneliness and, when her depression welled up to despair, led her to explore a range of ways of committing suicide, none of which she had so far put to the test. The confusion of which she complained appeared to result from the plethora of strong emotions that she was experiencing. (Viney, 1993, p. 114)

Because emotional reactions to an event increase the likelihood that an event will be remembered (Payne & Kensinger, 2010), what stories are important to clients and what stories clients will tell their therapists should be influenced by the type and intensity of affect associated with client stories. Similarly, what clients remember from therapy, both in session and outside of session, should be strongly influenced by the affect associated with therapy dialogs and events. These findings have implications for progress and outcome assessment in therapy: As clients' problems resolve, reports of NA should decrease in frequency and intensity (Meier & Vermeersch, 2007). Thus, one of the advantages for NA as a construct of interest for measurement is its universality. For most clients, an eventual decrease in the frequency and intensity of NA should indicate improvement in psychotherapy. By comparison, language and word use are marked by their uniqueness; the meaning an individual makes of and expresses about a particular situation typically differs significantly from other people, even people in similar situations. NA is more elemental.

Research also indicates that NA may be a key domain for the assessment of progress and outcome for most individuals participating in counseling and psychotherapy. Meier and Vermeersch (2007) summarized studies by Vermeersch, Lambert, and Burlingame (2000), Weinstock and Meier (2003), and Vermeersch et al. (2004), examining change across a range of problem domains in a total of 7,344 clients who received services at university counseling centers, an outpatient clinic, private practitioners, and employee assistance programs. While this sample contains a heterogeneous set of clients, presenting problems, therapists, and therapeutic interventions, Meier and Vermeersch (2007) found that depression and anxiety-related items evidenced larger effect sizes than items assessing other domains. While the presence of a therapeutic relationship and the establishment of hope may represent important *common process elements* (Wampold, 2001), these results suggest that depression and anxiety represent *common outcome elements*. That is, all interventions, regardless of theoretical orientation or client presenting problem, should produce improvements on outcome measures that contain NA content.

One novel measure for assessing NA is the Depression/Anxiety Negative Affect experimental scale (DANA; Meier, 2011). The DANA scale contains NA descriptors in five clusters representing increasing intensity of NA; the levels are 1, *Transient NA*; 2, *Increasing NA*; 3, *Moderate NA*; 4, *Intense NA*; and 5, *Extreme NA*. Figure 6.1 displays three of the five DANA levels; levels 1 and 5 represent the extremes of affective experiencing. By checking any item, the rater indicates that the client has experienced NA at the indicated level. This rating methodology allows the clinician to indicate an intensity level without the need for exact accuracy in terms of the specific NA term chosen (cf. Hesketh, Pryor, & Gleitzman, 1989).

Paul's (1986) Direct Observational Coding (DOC) procedures informed several aspects of DANA's construction. The general principle behind DOC procedures is that recording the presence or absence of a behavior enhances test score validity, while greater inference and interpretation

1. For each of the affective terms on the right, **check any that were salient** for this individual **over the past week**. If another term applies, please write it in the blank space.

Level 1 TRANSIENT NEGATIVE AFFECT

__ Bored	__ Unrelaxed
__ Preoccupied	__ Uncomfortable
__ Blue	__ Deflated

Level 3 MODERATE NEGATIVE AFFECT

__ Embarrassed	__ Worried
__ Pressured	__ Moderately angry
__ Anxious	__ Frustrated
__ Ruminating	__ Moderately sad
__ Scared	__ Agitated
__ Depressed	__ Distressed

2. At the **highest level** checked, **rate the frequency of the most frequently occurring term**.

How often experienced in past week?

1-2 days ⬭ *3 or more days* ⬭

Ever experienced more than 1x a day?

Yes ⬭ No ⬭

Level 5 EXTREME NEGATIVE AFFECT

__ Actively homicidal	__ Enraged
__ Actively suicidal	__ Despair
__ Bewildered	__ Panicked
__ Terrified	__ Traumatized
__ Intense guilt	__ Sobbing
__ ____________	

FIGURE 6.1 *DANA experimental scale.*

diminishes it. Consequently, rather than rate the frequency or intensity of NA terms with a multipoint rating scale (e.g., 1–5), which requires more judgment, DANA raters simply endorse an NA term if observed by the clinician or reported by the client. Raters also complete their NA assessments as soon as possible after a session to minimize memory errors. Paul (1986) noted that *reliability* of an observation decreases when the period between observation of a phenomena and the recording of the observation increases.

Evaluated in two outpatient samples where clinicians produce a total of 363 session ratings with 81 clients, DANA scores evidenced adequate internal consistency, support for discriminant and convergent *validity*, expected gender differences, and most importantly, *sensitivity to change* over the course of psychosocial interventions. Readers who would like more information about DANA should contact the author at stmeier@buffalo.edu.

Assessing Cognitions

Themes and Content

Because clinicians traditionally have kept written records of each therapy session (cf. American Psychological Association, 1993; Sommers-Flanagan & Sommers-Flanagan, 1999), psychotherapy progress notes represent a source of low-cost information that can be applied to narrative assessment. Little consensus exists about the content of such notes; they typically take the form of a general narrative or lists of important material (but compare Wiger's [1999] structured approach). Progress notes are used for a variety of purposes, including documenting service effectiveness, establishing baseline behaviors, and noting progress in relation to the treatment plan (Wiger, 1999).

One way to identify important data in progress notes is to borrow the analytic methods of qualitative research. Qualitative research focuses on the identification of important constructs, themes, and narratives contained in interviews or text (Creswell, 2007; Strauss & Corbin, 1997). Qualitative approaches share a common technique of rereading original material to note patterns and trends (Miles & Huberman, 1990). In a grounded theory analysis (Creswell, 2007; Strauss & Corbin, 1997), for example, the researcher identifies important concepts in field notes and then organizes them conceptually (Strauss & Corbin, 1997). Fitting well with narrative approaches, grounded theory takes a *constructivist perspective*, suggesting that individuals filter their versions of reality through the social meaning attributed to events and situations.

In a psychotherapy context, qualitative data in progress notes can be a key source of information, including causative process factors that influence client progress and outcomes (Meier, 2003). Themes, stories, issues, and metaphors can provide data about *process elements* and *outcome elements* in a *case conceptualization*. An anxious client, for example, might express that affective state by frequently switching topics within and between sessions. A recording of these topics per session could provide data about when, how often, and why the client switches issues, thereby deepening the case conceptualization and providing more information relevant for subsequent intervention.

Meier (1999, 2003) provided an example of the identification of important themes that emerged from qualitative analysis of progress notes from individual therapy with a depressed client. This information contains potentially important themes for elements of a case conceptualization. For example, the client's ideas about his role in the conflicted relationships of his family of origin and his continuing efforts to create a new family life appear to be important process elements (i.e., causative factors influencing progress and outcome). Similarly, the client's tendency to avoid processing of intense emotional material (and the resulting pace at which the therapist could effectively introduce this material) may be important for conceptualizing potential interventions. Table 6.3 summarizes important information related to progress and outcome with this client, with most of the important changes occurring later in therapy. As highlighted in the table, in Session 5, his anxiety is reported to have lessened considerably, while depression lessened moderately. Notes from Sessions 14 through 16 indicate that the client is contemplating significant changes to his primary relationship, work, and living arrangements. In Session 18, the client reports less guilt about his role in family conflict and less worrying and anger about his family (i.e., less NA). Finally, in Session 20, he concludes therapy by reporting greater self-confidence, emotional independence, and stable work performance.

Therapists and clinicians may employ a variety of analytic and graphical methods to perform analyses of qualitative data. Table 6.3 italicizes text to emphasize the status of outcome variables with this client; other information, such as NA, recurrent themes, or self-efficacy, could also be designated in progress notes. The therapist or client could also combine quantitative ratings (e.g., problem severity ratings, NA ratings) with qualitative information to juxtapose process and outcome information.

As clients make progress in therapy, previously repetitive themes should dissipate and clients should talk less about those topics (Madigan, 2011; Singer & Blagov, 2004; Teyber & McClure, 2011). Habermas et al. (2009), for example, conducted research that found that adult narratives of negative events were longer than narratives of positive events. Singer and Blagov (2004) described *repetitive memories* as repeated client reports that contain content related to important personal goals and issues; traumatic memories have been found to be repetitive in the sense that they repeatedly intrude into consciousness (Foa & Riggs, 1993). With effective therapy, what may have been a pressing topic when a client began therapy should lose its sense of urgency. Other topics may replace the presenting problem, but if the presenting problem has been resolved, the client should be less interested in talking about it. In general, a decrease in the presentation and length of discussion of a clinically relevant theme, as well as a decrease in negative affect around that theme, suggests that the client is ready for closure on these topics. If these topics are the primary focus of therapy, the client may also be ready for termination.

One assessment strategy is tracking the perseverance of client themes over time. Major themes or issues should have *persistent relevance* (Beutler & Hamblin, 1986), that is, the topic should appear repeatedly across sessions. As noted earlier, emotional reactions to an event increase the likelihood that an event will be remembered (Payne & Kensinger, 2010); consequently, as problems resolve and NA diminishes, clients should stop discussing the themes that they talked about earlier in therapy. Table 6.4, a variation of Table 3.1 in Chapter 3, is an example of what can be termed a *persistence*

TABLE 6.3 Qualitative Analysis of Progress Notes With an Individual Client

Session number	*Key issues*
1	Presenting problem centers on depression and anxiety; agrees to referral for possible medication; reports history of conflicted family relationships, particularly with long-deceased alcoholic father
2	Has started medication and will continue therapy; reports difficulty at work with "crazy" customers; we establish a schedule of activities designed to increase positive reinforcement for him
3	Reports a history of trying to recreate a family life, but with people other than immediate family of origin; for example, becomes a physical, emotional caretaker for distant relatives, older neighbors; reports no effect from reinforcement activities
4	Reports that he is very angry with many past incidents with family of origin, including father, and some current events with mother
5	*Much less anxious, moderately less depressed, but seems almost manic;* very strong emotional reactions to many current events
6	He agrees to start a journal where he writes thoughts, feelings, and related events
7	Reports that he has come to the conclusion that he hates himself; reading books about identity development; now frequent arguments with partner
8	Reports becoming easily angry with coworkers, even when their behavior does not affect him directly, as well as with partner and family members
9	Reads for 30 minutes from a journal about past family incidents that provoked anger, rage, and sadness in him; question arises whether he should pursue family therapy with mother and siblings
10	Notes that he is angry with his mother, but cannot express those feelings to her or even explore much in session; family culture indicates that being angry with parents is equivalent to disobeying them
11	Despite father's death 15 years ago, reports that he still wishes there was some way he could be emotionally close to father; I confronted him about this unrealistic idea; he later cancels next session

(*Continued*)

TABLE 6.3 Continued

Session number	*Key issues*
12	Some processing in session of how he experiences emotion; relates stories that provide evidence (to him) that his role was to function as emotional caretaker in his family; tried to protect mother from abusive, alcoholic father
13	No show; later reported that he forgot about the session
14	*Wondering whether to stay in current relationship*; debating financial security versus partner's treatment of him as a child
15	*Considering whether to leave town*, start a new life elsewhere; now spending much time considering therapy issues between sessions
16	Same issues as Session 15
17	Ran into his brother's friend who had no idea that client's father was alcoholic; confirmed for client that mother and siblings denied family difficulties; I noted that in the past he had denied such problems as well
18	Clearly has *changed locus of responsibility for family conflict away from himself; anger and rumination about family has decreased*; more focus on work, other people
19	Discusses buying a house with partner; one brother is now contacting him for social interactions
20	Termination; client reports *greater self-confidence, emotional independence from family, stable work performance; describes himself as "better integrated"*

Note: Italicized words indicate material relevant to outcome (Meier, 1999, 2003).

table, showing how themes for a client changed or persisted across five initial sessions. As shown in the table, a simple sum of the number of times a theme was discussed in session provides a rudimentary indication of the topic's importance for that client.

For this graduate student client, the two themes discussed most often were *funding concerns* and *stress over qualifying paper*, two relatively short-term stressors for the client. The NA states of anxiety, stress, and frustration were the major topics of Session 1, probably because they were the reasons motivating the client to attend therapy. These NA states were likely present in all subsequent sessions, but were less explicitly discussed because the major topics were the causes of the NA. New topics do appear and disappear over these sessions. For this client, short-term issues appear to be primary topics, but longer-term issues such as lack of motivation, where

TABLE 6.4 Persistence Table of Client Themes

Theme session	1	2	3	4	5	*Sum*
Anxiety and stress	×					1
Frustration	×					1
Stay here versus return to Argentina	×				×	2
Funding concerns	×	×	×	×		4
Lack of motivation	×			×		2
Racist comments		×				1
Social life		×		×		2
Interpersonal conflict		×	×			2
Stress over QP (qualifying paper)		×	×		×	3
Perfectionism			×			1
No balance			×			1
Romantic relationship				×		1
Lack of academic support			×		×	2
School ending					×	1
More productive weekend					×	1

Note: Funding concerns and Stress over QP are the 2 most frequently discussed topics by this client.

to live post graduation, and perfectionism are likely to return as topics in future sessions.

Self-Efficacy

Bandura (1977, 1997) provided detailed instructions for the development of quantitative tests to assess self-efficacy expectations for specific tasks. However, a therapist may decide to record self-efficacy qualitatively as part of progress notes. Guyker (2006), for example, described a 19-year-old Caucasian, heterosexual female who presented at a counseling center with mild depression after a series of academic and personal stressful events. The therapist conceptualized the client as having low self-efficacy for coping with interpersonal problems and a history of low self-esteem; these contributed to the client's ongoing anxiety and depression. Consequently, the therapist decided to track client statements related to self-efficacy for interpersonal problems (e.g., low assertiveness) and record these in progress notes for 10 therapy sessions. Table 6.5 displays examples of the identified self-efficacy themes and associated client statements.

TABLE 6.5 *Qualitative Analysis of Self-Efficacy Themes*

Session	*Themes and examples*
1	Ambivalence toward counseling
	"I know I should do this [counseling], so I'm glad I have to do it."
	Catastrophic thoughts
	"Everything [last semester] was just a mess."
	Difficulty in recalling self-involvement *(e.g., when asked about things that went well for client last semester, client reported, "I don't know. I don't really remember. I remember more about other people than myself.")*
2	Perception of inability to do something about an unfavorable situation
	"I just have to wait for him to bring it up."
3	Feelings of happiness when client acquired information by action-taking
	Self-report of feeling based on how people around her are doing
	"I'm really relieved that my problems aren't as bad as [my friend's]... makes me feel like everything I'm going through isn't really that bad."
4	Simply "going with the flow"
	Internal causal attribution
	"I was mean to him over break. That's probably why he didn't come around for a while ... I wonder how things would have been different over the past few months if I hadn't said all that."
	Fear of being put in a situation where she feels forced to say yes
	Reported habitual feeling of "not knowing"
5	Expressing happiness/satisfaction over being self-assertive and expressive of own feelings
6	Feeling that counseling has been helpful for her to stop and see what has gone on throughout week and being able to recognize her actions
	Admiration and attraction toward those who do possess self-confidence
	Hope that intoxication will help client express herself
7	Inability to recall how time is spent when client is not in class or at work
	Externalizing
	"I like to avoid drama, but I feel like it just finds me."

(Continued)

TABLE 6.5 Continued

Session	*Themes and examples*
8	Helplessness
9	Feeling like she has "bad luck" with situations, feeling like this is unfair and feeling a lack of control
10	Proactive, identification of areas for improvement, identification of own strengths

Note: Client themes are reported per session, with paraphrases of client quotes in italics.

Examination of the content of Table 6.5 suggests that the client frequently expressed a belief that important events in her life were out of her control. In Session 9, for example, she indicates that she has "bad luck" and "a lack of control." In initial sessions she indicates that she feels unable to do anything in unfavorable situations; she even has difficulty remembering events in which she participated. These descriptions suggest that concepts related to *locus of control* (Rotter, 1966) or a lack of *outcome expectations* (Bandura, 1977) might be better descriptions for this client than self-efficacy per se. Locus of control refers to whether a person believes they have the ability to influence or affect important events. For persons with an external locus of control (compared to an internal locus), luck and significant others have more influence than the individual. Outcome expectations are beliefs about what behaviors lead to desired outcomes. In this client's case, she appeared to believe that she had little influence with important persons and events in her life, beliefs worthy of further exploration in therapy.

Assessing Behavior

Verbal Behavior

Most psychotherapy theories focus on the use of specific words (e.g., word usage) or the meaning of the words used (e.g., themes) as markers for important constructs. Discussing the expression of shame in clients, Teyber and McClure (2011, p. 208), for example, suggested that:

> Clients directly reveal their shamed-based sense of self by repeatedly using words such as *bad, stupid, worthless, self-conscious, sheepish, embarrassed, low self-esteem, humiliated,* and so forth. Less direct indications of shame may include the repetitive use of words such as *should, ought to, must,* and *perfect*.

If psychotherapy is effective, verbal behavior should change. Metaphors, for example, can be tracked over time to determine if they reveal differences over time in how a client thinks and feels about a therapy issue. Levitt, Korman, and Angus (2000) found that in clients with depression who made improvements in therapy, their description of "being burdened" changed to "unloading the burden." No such change occurred in individuals who remained depressed.

Meier and Davis (2011, p. 26) provided an example of how a simple metaphor can be utilized to track a client's progress across sessions:

> ***Client:*** I'm making progress in therapy, but it is very difficult.
>
> ***Therapist:*** You're putting in a lot of effort.
>
> ***Client:*** Yeah ... it reminds me of a 15-round boxing match, and we're only in round 3.

Sport metaphors may provide fertile grounds for quantitative scoring and scaling of many client constructs, but their transparency also means that clients can easily over- or underreport information to fit personal biases.

Metaphors can also be a useful method of ascertaining the client's readiness to terminate. This example is from Viney (1993, p. 118) from a final session with a client who had previously introduced the "ship and crew" metaphor:

> ***Therapist:*** So I'm wondering whether you feel that you need me to help the process along, or whether you'd like to take off as captain of your own ship?
>
> ***Client:*** I would like to try and think as the captain ... but I know when I get into rough seas I'm going to need a good navigator.
>
> ***Therapist:*** I'm not suggesting that you should see somebody else at this stage or indeed that we should stop having these sessions ... but the end result of the sessions, that I want to see, is you out there as captain of your own ship.
>
> ***Client:*** Well, I think I'm ready for it. When I get into rough seas, I'll feel the need of some support. Will I be able to phone and make an appointment?

Pennebaker and colleagues have described a more structured approach to analysis of word usage. Based on the assumption that psychological information is conveyed through word use independent of semantic context (Pennebaker et al., 2003), computer-based word count systems analyze the content and style of word use to examine grammatical units (e.g., use of personal pronouns) as well as psychological dimensions (e.g., emotional words). *Linguistic Inquiry and Word Count* (LIWC; Pennebaker, Francis, & Booth, 2001) is a text analysis software for analyzing large archival datasets of text. LIWC analyzes differences in the extent to which people use different categories of words, including positive and negative emotions, self-references, and causality.

Word use research findings have implications for the identification of language markers for progress and outcome assessment in psychotherapy. First, measures administered during the beginning of therapy should indicate initial increases in or maintenance of higher levels of NA as the client expresses and experiences these states; this should certainly be the case for clients with internalizing disorders such as anxiety and depression. An increase in the use of different pronouns, indicating an understanding of different perspectives on a problematic situation, should also be associated with improvement in psychotherapy. Client statements indicating greater insight into problem causes and an increase in positive emotions should be more evident toward the middle and end of therapy. A reduction in the frequency of the telling of a problematic story or a story's problematic themes should be evident toward the end of successful therapy.

Self-Monitoring

With *self-monitoring*, clients record information about themselves outside of the therapy session (Craske & Tsao, 1999; Davis & Meier, 2011; Nelson, 1977). The client observes him- or herself on some dimension and records that information as it occurs, at the first available opportunity, or at the end of the day in a diary. The client then brings the resulting data for discussion at the next therapy session. From a narrative perspective, self-monitoring allows clients to check their self-descriptions with real-world, real-time data.

The type of information recorded usually relates to a specific problem or event the client has discussed (e.g., smoking cessation or panic attacks). That is, the information the client records is *idiographic* or specific to that person (i.e., the client wants to increase the number or length of study sessions). This enhances the client's motivation to perform the self-monitoring homework since the client is recording personally relevant behavior. While a specific behavior, such as the number of cigarettes smoked or the number of conversations initiated, is typically the focus of self-monitoring, the target of self-monitoring could also be thoughts or feelings. A client might record, for example, whenever she has an intrusive thought or a depressed feeling. In general, therapists should encourage clients to record data as soon as possible since memory errors are more likely to occur as the time between behavior and recording increases (Paul, 1986).

Self-monitoring has been shown to be a useful method for both assessment and intervention. Research indicates that recording of such behavioral problems as smoking decreases the observed behavior independent of other interventions (Nelson, 1977). Self-monitoring appears to be a *reactive* method of obtaining data: Because the individual becomes more aware of the observed behaviors, she or he is more likely to change those behaviors. And typically the behavior change is in a desired direction, such as decreased smoking or increased social interactions. As therapeutic homework, self-monitoring can be paired with graduated exposure to a feared or difficult situation. A college-aged client who describes being shy, for example, might agree to self-monitor the number of conversations he initiates with fellow students during the next week. If that number is zero, the homework for the following week might be to continue self-monitoring and also initiate at least one conversation, for any length of time.

Self-monitoring can be considered a structured method of being mindful. *Mindfulness* skills include psychological efforts to observe and describe events in a person's life, to participate with awareness (Linehan, 1993). This is also the core of any self-monitoring activity: Focusing on a problematic aspect of a person's life such as smoking or excessive drinking. Participating without awareness in such activities may be a key cause of impulsive behaviors (Linehan, 1993). Repeated use of any self-report measure may induce self-monitoring and mindfulness in the person completing the questions.

Assessing Obstacles to Change

Many of the methods previously described in this chapter may also be usefully applied to identify and assess obstacles to change. On a measure of NA, for example, clients will evidence a variety of patterns related to progress. Figure 6.2 displays patterns of actual clients who completed DANA as part of the test development; the data displayed are the highest intensity level rated per session. Client (a) evidences variable ratings over six sessions; these ratings may be indicative of a client who is cycling through high and low affect, similar to the cycles described by Mergenthaler (1996) of shifting between degrees of high and low emotion and high and low abstraction or reflection. Client (b), in contrast, shows lower NA during the first three sessions, but then escalates to the highest rated intensity in Sessions 4 and 5. One explanation for such a pattern is that the client underreported problems during the first sessions, but upon building trust in the therapist, reported the actual problems and associated NA severity. Indicating progress, Client (c) demonstrates straightforward decreases in NA over time. Finally, Client (d) displays relatively stable NA scores across sessions, with eventual improvement at the final rated session.

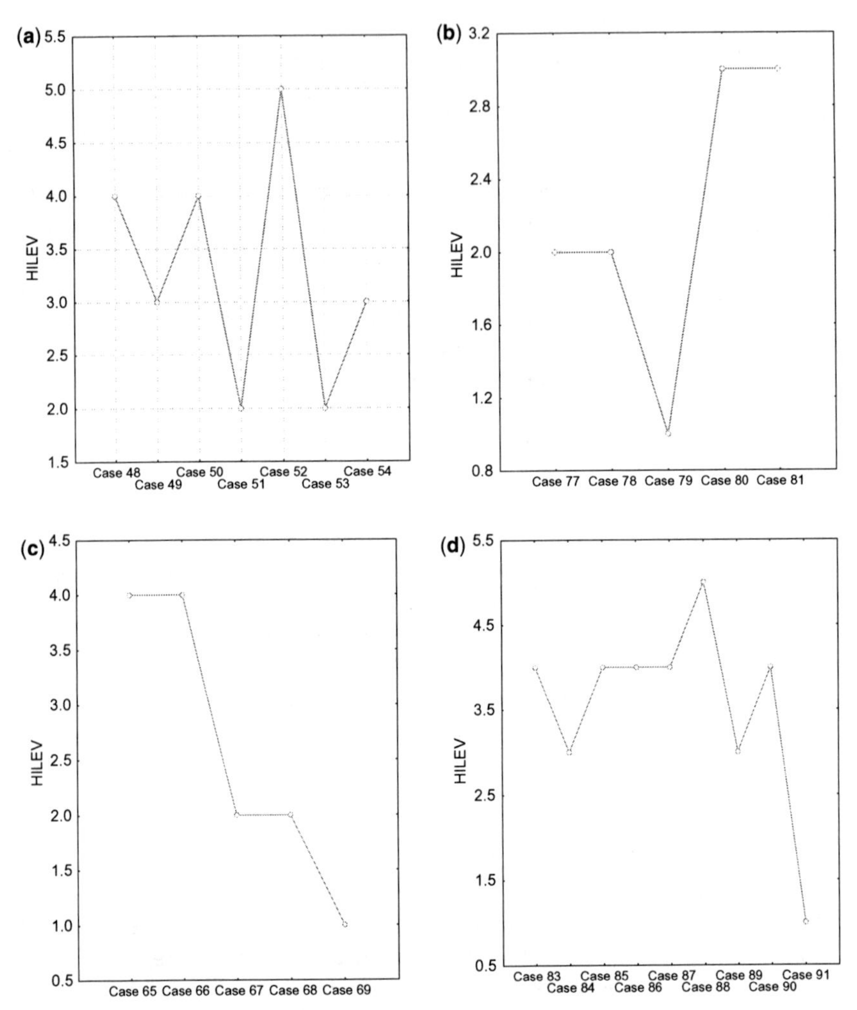

FIGURE 6.2 *DANA ratings for four clients.*
Note: *The graphs show change on DANA Highest Intensity Level (HILEV) for four clients. For the client depicted in (a), the displayed ratings begin at Intensity Level 4 (Intense NA) but range from Level 2 (Increasing NA) to 5 (Extreme NA), indicating a variable pattern. In (b), the clinical rater assessed this client at Intensity Level 1 (Transient NA) and 2 (Increasing NA) for the first three sessions, but in the following two sessions the HIL had increased to 4 (Intense NA), suggesting worsening. For the HIL ratings in (c), this client displays a ladder-step drop from Intensity Level 4 to Level 1, indicating improvement. Finally, the client in (d) evidences mostly stable HIL over eight sessions, then drops to Level 1 at the last rated session. Interpretation of all of these patterns requires knowledge of the client's psychological processes as reported and observed during therapy.*

Given that avoidance of NA often creates obstacles to processing affect, tracking NA across sessions can provide useful feedback to therapists, particularly in conjunction with tracking (via progress notes, for example) of session content. For Clients (a) and (b) in Figure 6.2, checking the content of progress notes for the sessions before and concurrent with worsening ratings may provide clues about what events were associated with these changes. Similar quantitative ratings of self-efficacy and other variables can be used to track progress and be juxtaposed with qualitative information to provide potential explanations for the observed data trends.

Client self-monitoring can be employed to track outcome variables such as number of cigarettes smoked or social interactions initiated, but clients may also usefully assess constructs related to obstacles. Thus, a client may record when ruminations occur to determine both frequency and potential antecedents and consequences. Similarly, counting avoidance behaviors may decrease their number as well as provide more information about when and why they occur. Similarly, one way to assess therapist-induced obstacles would be to compare the number of words spoken by therapists versus words spoken by client(s). Therapists should speak less over time, and exceptions to this case invite further scrutiny about the therapist's activeness; automated transcription services, as they become more widely available and affordable, make this type of analysis feasible.

SUMMARY AND IMPLICATIONS

In an important sense, language is the data of therapy. Verbal and nonverbal communications are the primary means of information transfer between therapist and client. Narrative elements are useful foci for progress and outcome assessment. So the meaning of stories and their building blocks (e.g., phrases, words, and descriptions) become potential units of interest for measurement as well as other narrative-related constructs such as NA, repetitive themes, metaphors, and descriptions of personal agency. This chapter briefly surveyed measurement and assessment methods related to these constructs. Readers may wish to review other potentially useful measures, including but not limited to the Experiencing Scale (Klein, Mathieu, Gendlin, & Kiesler, 1969; Klein, Mathieu-Coughlan, & Kiesler, 1986), repertory grid procedures (Jankowicz, 2003; Neimeyer, 1993; Neimeyer & Neimeyer, 1993), the Positive and Negative Affect Schedule (PANAS; Watson, Clark, & Tellegen, 1988), State-Trait Anxiety Inventory (STAI; Spielberger, Sydeman, Owen, & Marsh, 1997), and Beck Depression Inventory (BDI-II; Beck, Steer, & Brown, 1996).

In general, narrative and language studies suggest that client improvement is present when clients evidence more flexible behaviors, affect, and cognitions. Clients making progress may stop talking about a therapeutic theme, ruminate less, or talk about the topic less frequently or with less emotional intensity.

A significant obstacle to progress in psychotherapy practice and research remains the current status of psychological measurement and assessment (Meier, 1994, 2008b). Some observers have noted that qualitative analytic methods of narratives are subjective, can be biased, and are unsuitable for tasks such as word count and word classification (Pennebaker et al., 2003). In contrast, word count strategies are based on the assumption that psychological information is conveyed through word use, independent of semantic context (Pennebaker et al., 2003). Computer-based word count systems analyze the content and style of word use to examine grammatical units (e.g., use of personal pronouns) as well as psychological dimensions (e.g., emotions). Because the word count alternatives are computer-based, they require dictionaries and rules to sort and count words. To interpret the results of word count studies and to design more sophisticated dictionaries requires basic theories about the purpose of word use. As Pennebaker et al. (2003, p. 572) observed, "no one has yet devised a compelling psychological theory of word usage." Narrative concepts, however, appear poised to fill that void.

The ability to measure client progress well relates closely to the problem of *treatment failure*, which occurs when clients worsen or fail to make progress in therapy. Persons and Mikami (2002) noted that research estimates place the rate of treatment failure between 10% and 50% of all clients and that some studies suggest that 50% or more of psychotherapy participants do not improve. They also cautioned that "we have found in our caseloads, and we believe that readers who examine their own caseloads will also find, a surprising number of patients who have been in treatment for a disconcertingly long time without making significant progress" (Persons & Mikami, 2002, p. 143). A plausible explanation for these high failure rates is that therapists do not possess or employ systematic methods for obtaining feedback about clients' lack of progress (Clement, 1994). Hopefully, future psychotherapists will follow L'Abate's (2011, p. 228) belief that "any intervention without a before and after evaluation and follow-up is essentially unprofessional."

Seven

Future Directions, Briefly

NARRATIVES AS A UNIFYING MODEL AND METAPHOR

Whether the modality is individual, couple, family, or group, all psychotherapies depend upon narratives and language in the communication between therapist and client. Angus and McLeod (2004, pp. 373–374) summarized the case for narratives as the foundation for psychotherapy theories and inspiration for unifying the different branches:

> The concept of narrative is so fundamental to human psychological and social life ... that it provides a genuine meeting point between theoretical schools of therapy ... There has not been so far an integrative conceptualization of therapy that has captured the imagination of therapists and clients. While the common factors theory as an integrative model may be true, it seems to lack a generative spark. It has not inspired groundbreaking research or innovative practice. It does not have a creative edge. The concept of narrative ... is certainly creative and innovative. It may be the spark.

This push for integration is important because of the problems associated with a profession with more than 550 different types of psychotherapy (Kazdin, 2000). The most significant issue is that knowledge about psychotherapy continues to be organized in the form of lists of findings, with little connection or accumulation of results that could improve theory and practice.

Compared to more mature sciences, the rate of theoretical and scientific progress in counseling and psychotherapy is relatively slow. Arguments can be made that the knowledge base extends beyond common-sense folk psychology and that the field has considerable evidence for the general effectiveness of psychotherapy (e.g., Smith & Glass, 1977). Linehan (1993,

p. 220), however, provided a good example of the field's lack of progress when she wrote of the similarity of Dialectical Behavior Therapy (DBT) ideas of dialectics with previous approaches that "in a very real sense, the emphasis on dialectics in DBT is 'nothing new.'" McLeod (1997, p. ix) similarly concluded that "there are no new therapies." Clinical practice stagnates without new knowledge and improvements in assessment methods (Meier, 2008b). What early career clinicians see as innovative treatment approaches are often previously developed methods that have been slightly modified or even forgotten. Studying the career development of counselors, Ronnestad and Skovholt (2003, p. 26) found that experienced therapists often came to the conclusion that "there is a sense that there is not and will not be any significant new knowledge in the field."

I have taken the approach in this book that the field does not need yet another wave of new approaches. Rather, as a field we need to step back and integrate the considerable information we have learned to date, and develop new assessment methods that allow us to deepen what we know.

A NARRATIVE MODEL OF CHANGE

The narrative model of change described here functions as a parsimonious model of the essential elements of different systems of psychotherapy. As shown in Figure 7.1 (identical to Figure 1.2 in Chapter 1), these relatively few theoretical propositions offer the necessary guidelines for understanding much of what transpires during effective counseling and psychotherapy. That is, therapists work to provide effective therapeutic conditions that involve the client:

1. Paying attention to and experiencing the affect associated with the problems clients describe in their narratives.
2. Making sense of and finding meaning in the problem and associated affect.
3. Changing behavior to influence self-descriptions around personal agency related to client problems.
4. Managing the factor that interfere with the first three elements.

The psychotherapy field may be beginning to end the categorization phase of theory and research where major efforts have focused on parsing clinical problems (e.g., anxiety, eating disorders) by populations (e.g., gender, race/ethnicity). Some of this categorization may be driven by the fact that in quantitative studies, finding statistically significant effects is facilitated by the use of more homogeneous comparison groups. However, the field appears to be cycling back to the idea that similar approaches

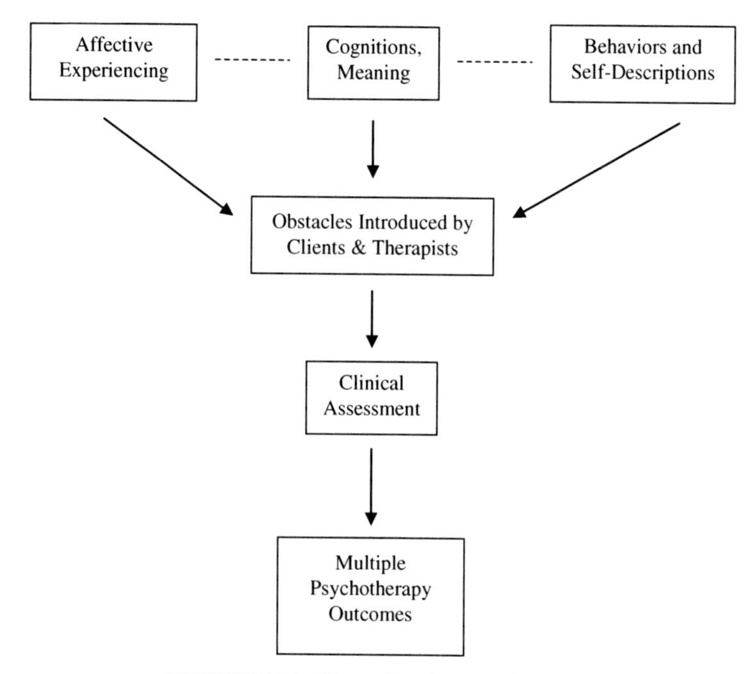

FIGURE 7.1 *Narrative theory of change.*

can be effective with different problems and populations. David Barlow, for example, has written several publications describing a unified approach to mental health problems (e.g., Campbell-Sills & Barlow, 2007; Moses & Barlow, 2006). Moses and Barlow (2006) noted that many clients present with high rates of comorbidity (e.g., persons with an anxiety disorder also have depression) and that treatment of an anxiety disorder typically leads to improvements in the other problems. Consequently, they describe a treatment approach that involves restructuring faulty cognitions, changing what they term emotion-driven behaviors, and facilitating emotional exposure and preventing emotional avoidance.

When describing a theory of change, attempts to go much beyond broad principles will be problematic. Individual clients vary greatly in response to psychotherapy, and much of what skilled clinicians do in practice is based on tacit knowledge accumulated through years of experience with a heterogeneous group of clients. To many psychotherapists, case studies and related stories carry more interest and perhaps, credibility, than do quantitative research studies. Because treatment manuals lack the specificity needed for dealing with individual cases, they should be considered as checklists. Similarly, *empirically validated treatments* have been relabeled *empirically supported treatments* to acknowledge the need to modify the procedures as therapy progresses with particular clients.

ADAPTING PSYCHOTHERAPY TO THE CLIENT: AN IDIOGRAPHIC FOCUS

Paul's (1967, p. 111) question of "*What* treatment, by *whom*, is most effective for *this* individual with that specific problem, under *which* set of circumstances?" had an enormous impact on researchers' thinking about how to evaluate the effectiveness of counseling and psychotherapy. In terms of research methodology, Paul essentially posed a question about independent variables (IVs), that is, the set of categories that researchers examine to identify what factors influence success in psychotherapy. The legacy of this question extends to current efforts to utilize research findings to establish empirically supported treatments and their accompanying treatment manuals.

While Paul's question has been enormously successful in framing research efforts, others have begun to describe its limitations. Kazdin (2000, p. 214), for example, observed that "this question is not very feasible or useful in light of the extraordinary number of treatments, disorders, and moderators ... The progress of psychotherapy *is* remarkable—the *remark* one is *able* to make is that very little has been achieved to date in understanding which treatments are effective." Psychotherapy researchers in fact have researched a very large number of potentially causative factors (Lambert, Garfield, & Bergin, 2004); many IVs, such as working alliance and severity of problem, have been found to have small to moderate effects on a variety of outcome measures. However, the relative importance of these factors, and how they interact, remain unclear, and the result is that researchers have created a long list of causative factors, with little connective theory.

Moreover, Paul's question misses elements that clinicians, and increasingly, researchers, believe to be key to understanding progress and failure in psychotherapy. Note that while the question focuses on an individual client, it is a client "with that specific problem" (Paul, 1967, p. 111). Essentially, the question does away with the specific client and replaces her/him with a diagnostic category or behavioral domain, "a specific problem." The implications of focusing on individuals (i.e., an idiographic perspective) versus groups of individuals (i.e., nomothetic) are important for thinking about the evaluation and practice of psychotherapy (Allport, 1937; Lamiell, 1990). Linehan (1993, p. 219) described the effects of this nomothetic thinking on clinical work:

> If a patient does not improve, there is something wrong with her rather than with the therapy. The patient is taught to fit the therapy; we do not ordinarily think of fitting the therapy to the patient.

The focus on what works with *groups* of individuals sharing a similar problem is important for policy issues. If an intervention has been shown to be effective, on average, in alleviating symptoms of persons with depression, for example, then it makes sense for insurers and government agencies to reimburse that treatment. But given that decades of psychotherapy research have demonstrated that individuals, even persons with the same problem, respond differently to a particular intervention, this research is of modest use to a clinician who sits facing a particular client. The clinician has no *a priori* way of knowing whether that specific person will benefit from, worsen, or stay the same with the research-supported therapy.

While nomothetic causes may be useful for the purposes of teaching and treatment planning, the treatment process is primarily idiographic and client-driven (Bohart & Tallman, 1999). The broad outlines of a generally effective approach can be sketched, with the responsibility for gaining experience with a broad set of heterogeneous clients falling on each clinical craftsperson. As Milton Erickson, cited in Zeig (1982, p. vii), put it:

> Each person is a unique individual. Hence, psychotherapy should be formulated to meet the uniqueness of the individual's needs, rather than tailoring the person to fit the Procrustean bed of a hypothetical theory of human behavior.

Similarly, Gonzalez (2001, p. 561) summarized Bohart and Tallman's (1999) conclusion that "therapists may activate the client's potential for self-healing by various interventions, but it is really a matter of the client making use of the interventions that constitutes the actual therapy." Indirect evidence certainly suggests that the therapist and provided interventions can make less difference than commonly assumed. Lambert (2005) noted that research methods examining dismantling and constructive strategies, where researchers attempt to isolate the effects of particular components of psychotherapy, typically do not find differences in outcome. Research also indicates that clients may report substantial improvements very early in therapy, before any psychotherapeutic intervention is expected to be effective (Kelly, Roberts, & Ciesla, 2005; Lambert, 2005). Clients do not stop processing therapeutically relevant information when they leave a session; in fact, most of their affective, cognitive, and behavior work is likely to be outside of session, in their daily lives.

The best psychotherapists may be professionals who start with a theoretically based, empirically supported theory of efficacious treatment and then adapt it to different clients. Experienced therapists build up a set of clinical experiences that enable them to recognize general patterns of psychological functioning in clients. The ability to recognize those patterns (e.g., the adolescent with severe eating disorder who resists hospitalization even when she intellectually sees the need), along with a repertoire of strategies for therapy process, becomes tacit knowledge for skilled therapists. Skilled therapists essentially learn to apply basic principles in the context of individual persons; over time, this sequence becomes automatic and turns into tacit knowledge that the clinician may have difficulty articulating (cf. Crawford, 2009). These ideas fit well with other approaches to psychotherapy that shift the locus of change away from therapist and intervention toward the client (e.g., Howard et al., 1996; Lambert, 2001; Shinn, 2007).

This idiographic concept also explains why many practicing clinicians describe themselves as eclectic in their approach. It is not only that skilled clinicians select one or more methods for a client, but also that they weave these approaches together, essentially creating a new therapy for each client. Just as with empirically supported treatments, however, therapists should not assume that each new approach, no matter how creative or insightful, will be successful with a client.

A FOCUS ON WHAT CHANGES IN PSYCHOTHERAPY

We know relatively little about what changes in or with the client during psychotherapy. Research suggests that different sorts of problems might be amenable to short- and long-term psychotherapy. In a study of SCL-90-R items (a symptom checklist) completed by psychotherapy outpatients, Kopta, Howard, Lowry, and Beutler (1994) found that the items could be grouped into three categories: (a) acute, that is, the items evidenced a quick response to treatment, (b) chronic distress, a moderate response rate, and (c) characterological, a slow response rate. Thus, clients reported relatively quick improvement on items assessing acute distress symptoms such as temper outbursts and hopelessness, whereas characterological items such as paranoia took longer to evidence change.

As described in Chapter 6, Meier and Vermeersch (2007) examined change on individual items of psychotherapy outcome measures in three outcome studies employing a total of 7,344 clients who received services at university counseling centers, an outpatient clinic, private practitioners, and employee assistance programs (Vermeersch et al., 2000; Vermeersch et al., 2004; Weinstock & Meier, 2003). While the psychotherapy literature indicates that nothing beyond a general positive improvement across domains should be present in such a heterogeneous dataset, Meier and Vermeersch (2007) found that depression and anxiety-related items evidenced larger effect sizes than items assessing other domains. They suggested that depression and anxiety, as negative affect (NA), may represent a *common outcome factor* related to NA and that alleviation of negative mood states may be a ubiquitous effect of all therapeutic interventions.

Somova and Meier (2009) examined the 20-item Behavioral Health Questionnaire's (BHQ) sensitivity to detecting change in a sample of 4,812 university counseling center clients who completed the measure after Sessions 1, 2, 3, and 6. Somova and Meier (2009) found that an item assessing distress ("How distressed have you been?") evidenced the largest change from Session 1 to Session 2. The distressed item's effect size (ES) of 0.58 was almost twice as large as the item with the next largest ES (feelings of sadness, ES = 0.35). This indicates that many clients experienced a rapid reduction in distress during initial sessions: While 55% of BHQ completers at Session 1 reported being extremely or very distressed, only 27–30% did so in Sessions 2, 3, and 6. Howard et al.'s (1996) phase theory indicates that this rapid change results from remoralization or installation of hope; in the phase model, measures of well-being should first evidence positive change, followed by stress reduction and life functioning (Kopta & Lowry, 2002).

The change processes and effects described in this chapter indicate that multiple pathways to positive outcomes exist. This may be another way to depict the process of being an eclectic therapist, that is, one adapts the theoretical model and empirically based techniques to fit the specific individual and unfolding treatment process. Crawford (2009, p. 168) quoted Klein as observing that "in many dynamic, uncertain, and fast-paced environments, there is no single right way to make decisions." In many clinical situations, ambiguity reigns, and what is needed is a method to ascertain whether progress is being made with whatever intervention(s) has been chosen.

WHAT CAN GO WRONG?

Employing a narrative and language model as a unifying theory does not mean that anything goes; the model does indicate that circumstances exist in which therapists will be ineffective. As noted in Chapter 5, labeling client *emotions* such as depression, anxiety, and stress as client *problems* can be misleading. That is, many clients will come to therapy and describe their presenting problem as "depression," that is, the feeling that distresses them. But depression may be a symptom, not a cause, and so it is not the depression that should be the target of therapeutic intervention but the causes. While the depression may need to be experienced fully as part of the therapeutic process, the causes of the depression may be a difficult job, loss of relationship, or other stressful situations. In other cases, clients' thinking about their affective states may make those feelings into a problem. Good examples are individuals with panic disorders whose anxiety is accelerated in intensity in response to an awareness of being anxious or having a physical symptom such as chest pain (Tull & Roemer, 2007).

Treating affective, cognitive, and behavioral aspects of narratives as separate elements is an intellectual convenience. A close reading of the principles described in Chapters 2 through 4 indicates that at least two elements, and usually all three, must be addressed for effective clinical work. Rumination, for example, is often associated with avoidance of affective experiencing and failing to perform feared behaviors in difficult situations. The narrative model suggests that therapists who focus their interventions on only one client modality—affect, cognition, or behavior—will be less effective than therapists who move across these domains with each client. A therapist who focuses only on behavior change will likely facilitate fewer beneficial outcomes with the substantial set of clients who would also benefit from affective processing and meaning-making related to their presenting problem(s). Similarly, a therapist who focuses only on insight and meaning-making will be less effective with clients whose presenting problem(s) require affective processing and work with new behaviors. These imbalanced approaches, however, may still produce benefits, owing to personality and other factors whereby clients pursue the complementary modes outside of session and independent of the therapist's intended interventions.

Finally, given the broad description of the change process in the narrative model, and the need to adjust therapy to adapt to the variations in therapeutic process introduced by individual clients, the therapist cannot simply depend on clinical judgment to track therapy progress. As described in Chapter 5, many clients present obstacles during the therapy process. The result is that while some clients will respond quickly and positively to therapy, others will worsen, show considerable variability before achieving stable positive change, or simply show no change over time. Most therapists act as if they can informally track clients' patterns of change, but research suggests that many therapists, with many clients, are not accurate assessors of client progress, especially if the client is failing to make progress (Gray & Lambert, 2001). Therapists need more structured methods to track progress and outcome if they wish to avoid treatment failure and improve their rates of positive outcomes (Harmon, Hawkins, Lambert, Slade, & Whipple, 2005).

FUTURE RESEARCH

An approach to therapy that focuses on language appears to arrive, and eventually fade away, every few decades. In the 1970s and 1980s neurolinguistic programming (NLP; Bandler & Grinder, 1979) was a popular therapy that heavily utilized storytelling and metaphors. However, many of its tenets did not receive research support or were not evaluated from a research perspective. Given the relatedness of NLP and contemporary approaches to narrative therapies, this history provides cause for skepticism about the effectiveness of narrative therapies. This concern is heightened by some contemporary narrative therapists' disinterest in or open antagonism toward research evaluations of narrative work.

Research is needed to determine if therapists with more successful clients differ in their use of narrative and language compared to less successful therapists. Therapists of successful clients, for example, may do a better job of matching their clients in terms of the client's reading level, cognitive complexity, or the intensity level of NA discussed in session. Similarly, if therapists-in-training show differences compared to experienced, successful therapists, studies of word use and narratives may provide useful information for therapist training programs. Do therapists-in-training, for example, use fewer words over time, or focus more on NA, as they become more experienced?

The idiographic emphasis of the narrative model described here suggests that client characteristics related to language and narratives are worthy of considerable study. How does client language, for example, indicate the degree of NA intensity the client is comfortable with? Do recurrent themes decrease over time as clients successfully conclude therapy? Does any commonality across clients exist in terms of how client language related to self-efficacy changes over time in successful cases?

Finally, the most important area for future research (and needed grant support) is measurement and assessment of language- and narrative-related constructs. While the key to successful real estate purchases may be location, location, location, the key to progress in developing psychotherapy as a science is *assessment, assessment, assessment*. Almost all funded research related to psychotherapy focuses on intervention, with little investment in studying *how* we should determine *what* changes in psychotherapy. This is putting the cart before the horse, and at some point the field needs support for conducting research into basic science questions focused on the measurement of the effects of psychotherapy. Progress and outcome assessments of client narratives, based on measures including NA, story characteristics, self-efficacy, and client word use, are potentially fruitful grounds for further investigation.

Glossary

Anxiety In contrast to depression, anxiety is future focused. Bandura (1977, p. 137) defined anxiety as "a state of anticipatory apprehension over possible deleterious happenings."

Assessment A human judge's combination of data from tests, interviews, observation, and other sources. Assessment is a broader term than measurement or testing, and includes any measurement method that involves human judgment. In a clinical or psychological context, assessment information can include a history of the presenting problems, family background and social supports, current medical problems, education, current employment, and financial resources.

Assessment method Source or device employed to gather clinical data. These include self-reports, interviews, ratings by others, cognitive ability, and neuropsychological tests.

Avoidance Actions people take to evade a feared event or situation; the event or situation can also be an internal thought or feeling the individual wishes to avoid. Avoidance behaviors maintain anxiety by keeping the individual from exposure and eventual habituation to what currently may be safe situations, or difficult situations that the individual could learn to manage.

Case conceptualization Method for describing the important elements influencing a client.

Catastrophizing Instances when negative consequences of an event are exaggerated and one's ability to handle those consequences are underestimated.

Chronicles Stories or reports told with no sense of drama or purpose.

Clinically relevant feedback Process of obtaining and employing data about a client (often in regard to client progress) for use with the therapist and/or client to make adjustments in the provided therapy. Compare *patient-focused research*.

Common outcome elements Client symptoms that may show improvement for all or most clients regardless of intervention type. Negative affect, including anxiety and depression, is an example.

Common process elements Characteristics of therapy that may influence progress for all clients, regardless of intervention type. Examples include the quality of the therapeutic relationship and the establishment of hope.

Compacted phrase Short phrase or sentence that clients employ repeatedly to communicate their emotional reaction to stressful events. Example phrases include "It's too much for me; I can't stand it."

Constellations of feelings Basic emotions that are linked and typically occur in a predictable sequence. Teyber and McClure (2011) suggested that common groupings are anger–sadness–shame and sadness–anger–guilt.

Constructivist perspective Individuals filter perceptions through the social meaning attributed to events and situations. Thus, most events will likely have different meanings for different people.

Context Background, situation, or environment in which some action or event takes place. Context is always important in terms of understanding a client's meaning, affect, and behavior.

Corrective emotional experience Creation of a working alliance and emotionally healthy relationship between therapist and client. This relationship corrects the client's previous understandings of a normal relationship, typically built on experiences with parents and other significant persons in the client's life.

Countertransference Broadly, feelings the therapist has about the client.

Critical theory Different ideologies (e.g., political, cultural, economic) distort apparent reality, particularly for and about oppressed groups. Glesne (2011, p. 10) noted that "critical theory researchers see research as a political act because it not only relies on value systems, but challenges value systems."

Cultural background Aspects of a client's life history, such as culture, ethnicity, and gender, that may influence how they perceive the therapy process.

Cultural narratives Stories of the good life, for a particular culture.

Deconstruction Process in which therapists help clients become aware of the dominant story that guides their lives and to question its themes so that the story becomes just one possible view of the self.

Defensive deniers Individuals who deny or repress negative feelings, instead reporting positive mental health.

Deletions Distortion where individuals selectively focus on certain aspects of the environment and ignore other elements.

Depression Feelings of sadness triggered by past events such as a significant loss.

Dialectics Process of reconciling opposites through synthesis.

Dysnarrativia Impairment in the ability to tell or understand stories; sense of self lost.

Emotional processing Subjective experience of holding a feeling in awareness. If the feeling is experienced long enough, it typically decreases in intensity.

Emotion schemas Individual differences in how people think about their emotions as well as the situations that elicited the emotions.

Environment Situation or context in which a client acts. Can refer to an environment as perceived by the client or by a group of individuals (the two perceptions can and usually do differ).

Excluded experiences Elements of a person's life that are not included in personal narratives.

Exploration phase Beginning phase of therapy where clients provide their initial narratives about clinical therapy; some clients may minimize problems or present less serious problems initially.

Externalizing Separating the person from the problem; one option is to discuss the problem as if it were situated outside the person's body or mind.

Generalizations Specific ideas about the world or how individuals operate in it that are untrue beyond particular circumstances.

Homework Assigned activities and tasks that clients perform outside of the therapy session.

Hypothesis Confirmation Bias (HCB) Tendency to crystallize on early impressions and ignore later information that contradicts the initial hypothesis.

Identified patient Individual who is referred for therapy. Individuals in a system (e.g., family, organization) consider the identified patient to be problematic or the source of problems in the system.

Idiographic Information specific to a particular individual; principles related to individuals, as compared to a nomothetic understanding of a group of people.

Ill-formed or incomplete statements Aspects of narratives or language use that distort or omit important material.

Illusions A belief or dream that does not match current information about a person's capabilities or aspects of the environment in which the person lives.

Implication Additional information beyond that contained in the content of speech or text.

Integrative statement Report of lessons learned from life experiences.

Intellectualization Tendency for some clients to stay at a cognitive level and fail to pay attention to or process affect.

Irrational belief A personal belief that is not supported by evidence.

Leagues Groups of individuals (typically clients or persons with experience with the relevant issue or problem) who work together to educate and influence public perceptions and policy about a mental health issue.

Linguistic Inquiry and Word Count Text analysis software for analyzing archival datasets of text. Results indicate the extent to which individuals employ different categories (e.g., emotions, self-references) of word use in their speech.

Locus of control Whether a person believes if one has the ability to influence or affect important life events. Persons with an external locus of control believe that the control lies outside of their influence, while persons with internal locus of control expect to be able to influence significant life events.

Logical positivism Philosophical position based on the concept that an objective reality exists.

Macronarratives The client's life story.

Manualized therapy Procedures for working with a client with a specific problem, with the procedures listed in a treatment manual. Typically, the procedures are research-based, that is, they have been evaluated by empirical research.

Meaning-making Process of making sense of an emotionally disturbing event.

Metaphor Figure of speech that compares one thing to another. Typically, the source domain is a more concrete concept and the target domain a more abstract idea. Source domains include basic topics such as the body, animals, buildings, temperature, and food (Kovecses, 2002).

Micronarratives Stories told in the therapy hour.

Mindfulness A set of skills intended to help a person participate with awareness in an activity. Participating without awareness is assumed to be key to impulsive behaviors (Linehan, 1993).

Multiple fragmented identities Self-descriptions that are incompatible with each other in the person's life stories.

Negative affect A feeling subjectively experienced as unpleasant or aversive.

News of difference Bateson's (1979) idea that all information depends on the perception of differences and that this perception triggers all new responses in living systems.

Nonverbal communication Information conveyed by a person through any means besides the content of speech. Examples include tone of voice, facial expressions, hand movement, and body posture.

Open-ended questions Questions that cannot be answered with one or two words, which can logically answer a closed-ended question. An example of a closed-ended question is "Is it raining outside?" An example of an open-ended question is, "How do you feel about starting therapy?"

Outcome elements Component(s) in a case conceptualization that relate to symptoms and effects of the client's problem(s).

Outcome expectations Beliefs about which behaviors will produce desired outcomes or avoid unwanted outcomes.

Pacing and leading Process of the therapist's statements matching client content before introducing new information or content.

Patient-focused research Study that focuses on providing therapists with direct feedback about a client's progress. The therapist can use the feedback to adjust therapeutic interventions as needed.

Persistence table Table displaying a matrix of client themes discussed by session number. Inspection of the table provides information about the persistent relevance of the topics discussed.

Persistent relevance Question of whether a problem or a set of problems a client presents at the beginning of therapy continues to be important in subsequent sessions. Clients, for example, may first describe relatively minor issues (e.g., a problem with a roommate) before later revealing a more socially undesirable problem (e.g., a drug addiction).

Positive affect A feeling subjectively experienced as pleasant.

Postmodernism Philosophical position that argues that no universal truths exist and that researchers must be grounded by their historical and local contexts.

Primary emotional reactions Emotions function as a signal of a person's situation in an environment. Contrast with secondary emotional reaction. For example, a person may experience grief at the loss of a loved one.

Probability overestimation Occurs when the likelihood of a feared event is exaggerated in client accounts.

Problem location Whether the client's problem is considered to be located within the person (i.e., their body/mind) or external to their person (conceptually). So, while we typically think of a state such as anxiety as within our self, it can be useful to think of the anxiety as an entity external to our body, as a thing of itself.

Problem solving Any effort to cope with or solve some personal difficulty. Typically conceived of as a cognitive activity.

Process elements In a case conceptualization, the causes and etiology of a client's problems.

Progress notes Qualitative written summary relevant to a client's therapy issues. Therapists typically write such notes after each therapy session, although the content of the note may be idiosyncratic to the particular therapist.

Psychological test Tools or systematic procedures for observing some aspect of human behavior and describing it with a numerical scale or category system. Tests are employed to produce a description of characteristics of individuals or groups.

Qualitative data Non-numerical data such as text and speech. Client progress notes are one example of qualitative data typically produced in psychotherapy.

Quantitative data Numerical information produced by psychological tests and assessment methods. A GRE score is one example of quantitative data.

Rebound effect Instance where the suppression of thoughts and feelings leads to an increase in those thoughts and feelings.

Reliability The consistency of scores on a measurement device. An intelligence test, for example, is expected to produce scores for individuals that remain largely stable over time.

Remoralization A client's restoration of hope.

Repetitive memories Remembering past events repeatedly, typically without conscious volition.

Reports Stories or chronicles told with no sense of drama or purpose.

Resistance Obstacles created by the client, often unconsciously, to resolving their problem. Resistance typically has a self-protective function.

Role-play Activity in which a client and therapist act out a (informal) script about a problematic situation in the client's life, typically involving other people.

Rumination Client thinking about a problem in which thoughts appear without the client's intent. The client has difficulty voluntarily stopping the ruminating thoughts.

Secondary emotional reaction Clients' response to their appraisal of a primary emotional reaction to their status in an environment. For example, an individual may notice they are experiencing grief because of a loss of a loved one, and then begin to feel anxiety when they anticipate another possible loss.

Self-defensive strategies Efforts to cope with intrusive memories and associated intense negative affect. That is, individuals may be motivated to avoid recalling and describing intensely aversive events and situations.

Self-defining memories Main elements of personality and identity, including personal goals.

Self-descriptions Aspects of client narratives that pertain to the client, as opposed to other people.

Self-disclosure Personal statements by the therapist about her- or himself related to the client. With a grieving client, for example, a therapist might say, "I also felt sad when my mother died." Contrast with self-involving statements by the therapist, which keeps the client's attention on him- or herself.

Self-efficacy expectations Description of personal competence for performing specific behaviors.

Self-involving statements Personal statements by the therapist about some important aspect of the client. A therapist might say, for example,

"I felt sad when you discussed how your mother died." Contrast with self-disclosure by the therapist, which turns the client's attention to the therapist.

Self-monitoring Outside of the therapy session, the client observes him- or herself on some dimension and records that information as it occurs, at the first available opportunity, or at the end of the day in a diary. The client then brings the resulting data for discussion at the next therapy session.

Self-report A method of obtaining data in which a person/client describes her- or himself on some dimension (e.g., self-description of level of anxiety).

Semiotics The study of signs and sign processes. From a narrative perspective, language is a sign system that represents something else.

Sensitivity to change A measurement method's ability to detect change over time on some psychological characteristic. Therapists typically are interested in learning if clients show change as a result of a psychosocial intervention, but the methods to detect such change can be problematic.

Social justice Study of social contexts that influence human rights.

States Changing characteristics of a person (e.g., mood) that are amenable to psychosocial intervention.

Suppression Efforts to hide one's feelings from oneself and/or others. Suppression often leads to a rebound effect, where the suppressed thoughts and feelings increase.

Therapeutic documents Any written document created for a therapeutic effect. White and Epston (1990), for example, described the use of letters of invitation to engage individuals reluctant to attend therapy.

Traits Enduring psychological characteristics of a person (e.g., neuroticism or extroversion), thought to be relatively stable over time for adults and situations. Traits are generally not amenable to psychosocial interventions, at least those that are short-term.

Treatment failure Generally refers to instances when clients fail to improve in therapy or worsen over the course of therapy. Literature contains different definitions of what constitutes failure in therapy.

Unique outcomes Neglected or forgotten aspects of clients' lives. These are surprising exceptions to the problem as described in the client's usual narrative.

Universal basic emotions Feelings common to all humans, such as anger, sadness, fear, and joy.

Validity Referring to measurement, two definitions are typically used: (a) whether a test measures what it is intended to measure, and (b) the inferences or purposes for which test scores can be employed.

Verbalization of affect Client translates bodily sensations and feelings into verbal language.

References

Abramowitz, J. S. (2002). Treatment of obsessive thoughts and cognitive rituals using exposure and response prevention: A case study. *Clinical Case Studies, 1*, 6–24. doi: 10.1177/1534650102001001002

Ahmed, M., & Boisvert, C. M. (2003). Enhancing communication through visual aids in clinical practice. *American Psychologist, 58*, 816–817. doi: 10.1037/0003-066X.58.10.816

Alberti, R. E. (2011). Helping others deal with the "new assertive you." In H. Rosenthal (Ed.), *Favorite counseling and therapy homework assignments* (pp. 33–37). New York: Routledge.

Alexander Street Press. (2009). Counseling and Psychotherapy Transcripts, Client Narratives, and Reference Works database. Retrieved from http://www.alexanderstreet.com

Allport, G. W. (1937). *Personality: A psychological interpretation.* New York: H. Holt and Co.

American Psychiatric Association. (2000). *Diagnostic and statistical manual of mental disorders* (4th ed., text rev.). Washington, DC: Author.

American Psychological Association. (1993). Record keeping guidelines. *American Psychologist, 48*, 984–986.

American Psychological Association. (1996). *Responding therapeutically to patient expression of sexual attraction (videotape)*. Washington, DC: Author.

Amir, N., Stafford, J., Freshman, M. S., & Foa, E. B. (1998). Relationship between trauma narratives and trauma pathology. *Journal of Traumatic Stress, 11*, 385–392. doi: 10.1023/A:1024415523495

Anderson, T. (2004). "To tell my story": Configuring interpersonal relations within narrative process. In L. E. Angus & J. McLeod (Eds.), *The handbook of narrative and psychotherapy* (pp. 315–329). Thousand Oaks, CA: Sage Publications.

Anderson, H., & Goolishian, H. (1990). Beyond cybernetics: Comments on Atkinson and Heath's "Further thoughts on second-order family therapy." *Family Process, 29*, 157–163.

Angus, L., Levitt, H., & Hardtke, K. (1999). The narrative processes coding system: Research applications and implications for psychotherapy practice. *Journal of Clinical Psychology, 55,* 1255–1270. doi: 10.1002/(SICI)1097-4679(199910)55:103.0.CO;2-F

Angus, L. E., & McLeod, J. (2004). Toward an integrative framework for understanding the role of narrative in the psychotherapy process. In L. E. Angus & J. McLeod (Eds.), *The handbook of narrative and psychotherapy* (pp. 367–374). Thousand Oaks, CA: Sage Publications.

Arkowitz, H., Westra, H. A., Miller, W. R., & Rollnick, S. (Eds.) (2008). *Motivational interviewing in the treatment of psychological problems.* New York: Guilford Press.

Arlow, J. A. (1979). Metaphor and the psychoanalytic situation. *The Psychoanalytic Quarterly, 48,* 363–385.

Bandler, R., & Grinder, J. (1975). *The structure of magic I: A book about language and therapy.* Palo Alto, CA: Science and Behavior Books.

Bandler, R., & Grinder, J. (1979). *Frogs into princes: Neurolinguistic programming.* Moab, UT: Real People Press.

Bandura, A. (1977). Self-efficacy: Toward a unifying theory of behavioral change. *Psychological Review, 84,* 191–215. doi: 10.1037//0033-295X.84.2.191

Bandura, A. (1986). *Social foundations of thought and action: A social cognitive theory.* Englewood Cliffs, NJ: Prentice Hall.

Bandura, A. (1997). *Self-efficacy: The exercise of control.* New York: W.H. Freeman.

Barker, P. (1985). *Using metaphors in psychotherapy.* New York: Brunner/Mazel.

Barlow, D., Farcione, T., Fairholme, C., Ellard, K., Boisseau, C., Allen, L., & Ehrenreich-May, J. (2011). *Unified protocol for transdiagnostic treatment of emotional disorders.* Oxford, UK: Oxford University Press.

Barlow, D. H. (1988). *Anxiety and its disorders: The nature and treatment of anxiety and panic.* New York: Guilford Press.

Barney, C., & Shea, S. (2007). The art of effectively teaching clinical interviewing skills using role-playing: A primer. *Psychiatric Clinics of North America, 30,* E31–E50. doi: 10.1016/j.psc.2007.03.001

Barrett, L. F. (2006). Are emotions natural kinds? *Perspectives on Psychological Science, 1*(1), 28–58.

Bateson, G. (1979). *Mind and nature.* New York: E.P. Dutton.

Battle, C., Imber, S. D., Hoehn-Saric, R., Stone, A. R., Nash, E. R., & Frank, J. D. (1966). Target complaints as criteria of improvement. *American Journal of Psychotherapy, 20,* 184–192.

Bauer, J., & Bonanno, G. A. (2001). I can, I do, I am: The narrative differentiation of self-efficacy and other self-evaluations while adapting to bereavement. *Journal of Research in Personality, 35*, 424–448. doi: 10.1006/jrpe.2001.2323

Beck, A. (1979). *Cognitive therapies and the emotional disorders*. New York: International Universities Press.

Beck, A., & Steer, R. A. (1987). *Manual for the revised Beck Depression Inventory*. San Antonio, TX: Psychological Corporation.

Beck, A., Steer, R. A., & Brown, G. (1996). *Manual for the revised Beck Depression Inventory-II*. San Antonio, TX: Psychological Corporation.

Beck, A. T., Emery, G., & Greenberg, R. L. (2005). *Anxiety disorders and phobias: A cognitive perspective*. New York: Basic Books.

Berman, P. (1997). *Case conceptualization and treatment planning*. Thousand Oaks, CA: Sage Publications.

Berntsen, D. (2010). The unbidden past: Involuntary autobiographical memories as a basic mode of remembering. *Current Directions in Psychological Science, 19*, 138–142. doi: 10.1177/0963721410370301

Beutler, L. E., & Hamblin, D. L. (1986). Individualized outcome measures of internal change: Methodological considerations. *Journal of Consulting and Clinical Psychology, 54*, 48–53. doi: 10.1037/0022-006X.54.1.48

Beutler, L. E., & Harwood, T. M. (2000). *Prescriptive psychotherapy: A practical guide to systematic treatment selection*. Oxford, UK: Oxford University Press.

Bliese, P. D., Wright, K. M., Adler, A. B., Thomas, J. L., & Hoge, C. W. (2007). Timing of postcombat mental health assessments. *Psychological Services, 4*, 141–148. doi: 10.1037/1541–1559.4.3.141

Bohart, K., & Tallman, K. (1999). *How clients make therapy work: The process of active self-healing*. Washington, DC: American Psychological Association.

Boothe, B., & Von Wyl, A. (2004). Story dramaturgy and personal conflict. In L. E. Angus & J. McLeod (Eds.), *The handbook of narrative and psychotherapy* (pp. 283–296). Thousand Oaks, CA: Sage.

Breitbart, W., & Heller, K. S. (2003). Reframing hope: Meaning-centered care for patients near the end of life. *Journal of Palliative Medicine, 6*, 979–988. doi: 10.1089/109662103322654901

Bruner, J. (1990). *Acts of meaning*. Cambridge, MA: Harvard University Press.

Bruner, J. (2004). The narrative creation of self. In L. E. Angus & J. McLeod (Eds.), *The handbook of narrative and psychotherapy* (pp. 3–14). Thousand Oaks, CA: Sage Publications.

Campbell, R. S., & Pennebaker, J. W. (2003). The secret life of pronouns: Flexibility in writing style and physical health. *Psychological Science, 14*, 60–65. doi: 10.1111/1467-9280.01419

Campbell-Sills, L., & Barlow, D. H. (2007). Incorporating emotion regulation into conceptualizations and treatments of anxiety and mood disorders. In J. J. Gross (Ed.), *Handbook of emotion regulation* (pp. 542–559). New York: Guilford.

Carlson, J., & Englar-Carlson, M. (2011). Series preface. In S. Madigan, *Narrative therapy*. Washington, DC: American Psychological Association.

Carter, R. T. (2007). Racism and psychological emotional injury: Recognizing and assessing race-based traumatic stress. *The Counseling Psychologist, 35*, 13–105. doi: 10.1177/0011000006292033

Castonguay, L., Pincus, A., Agras, W., & Hines, C. (1998). The role of emotion in group cognitive-behavioral therapy for binge eating disorder: When things have to feel worse before they get better. *Psychotherapy Research, 8*, 225–238.

Castonguay, L. G., Goldfried, M. R., Wiser, S., Raue, P. J., & Hayes, A. H. (1996). Predicting the effect of cognitive therapy for depression: A study of unique and common factors. *Journal of Consulting and Clinical Psychology, 64*, 497–504. doi: 10.1037//0022-006X.64.3.497

Chandler, D. (2007). *Semiotics: The basics*. London: Routledge.

Cirillo, L., & Crider, C. (1995). Distinctive therapeutic uses of metaphor. *Psychotherapy: Theory, Research, Practice, Training, 32*, 511–519. doi: 10.1037/0033-3204.32.4.511

Claiborn, C. D., & Goodyear, R. K. (2005). Feedback in therapy. *Journal of Clinical Psychology, 61*, 209–217.

Clement, P. W. (1994). Quantitative evaluation of 26 years of private practice. *Professional Psychology: Research and Practice, 25*, 173–176. doi: 10.1037//0735-7028.25.2.173

Clement, P. W. (1999). *Outcomes and incomes*. New York: Guilford.

Cone, J. D. (1988). Psychometric considerations and the multiple models of behavioral assessment. In A. S. Bellack & M. Hersen (Eds.), *Behavioral assessment: A practical handbook* (3rd ed., pp. 42–66). Elmsford, NY: Pergamon Press.

Cone, J. D., & Foster, S. L. (1991). Training in measurement: Always the bridesmaid. *American Psychologist, 46*, 653–654. doi: 10.1037//0003-066X.46.6.653

Corcoran, K., & Gingerich, W. J. (1994). Practice evaluation in the context of managed care: Case-recording methods for quality assurance reviews. *Research on Social Work Practice, 4*, 326–337. doi: 10.1177/104973159400400304

Corsini, R., & Wedding, D. (2007). *Current psychotherapies* (8th ed.). Pacific Grove, CA: Brooks/Cole.

Craske, M. (1999). *Anxiety disorders: Psychological approaches to theory and treatment.* Boulder, CO: Westview Press.

Craske, M., & Tsao, J. (1999). Self-monitoring with panic and anxiety disorders. *Psychological Assessment, 11,* 466–479. doi: 10.1037//1040-3590.11.4.466

Crawford, M. B. (2009). *Shop class as soulcraft: An inquiry into the value of work.* New York: Penguin Press.

Creswell, J. W. (2007). *Educational research* (3rd ed.). Upper Saddle River, NJ: Merrill Prentice Hall.

Cross, K. P., & Angelo, T. A. (1988). *Classroom assessment techniques: A handbook for faculty.* Ann Arbor, MI: National Center for Research to Improve Post-secondary Teaching and Learning.

Csikszentmihaly, M. (1993). *The evolving self: A psychology for the third millennium.* New York: Harper Collins.

Cummings, A. L., Hallberg, E. T., Slemon, A., & Martin, J. (1992). Participants' memories for therapeutic events and ratings of session effectiveness. *Journal of Cognitive Psychotherapy, 6,* 113–124.

Damasio, A. (1999). *The feeling of what happens.* New York: Harcourt Brace.

Davis, S., & Meier, S. (2001). *The elements of managed care: A guide for helping professionals.* Pacific Grove, CA: Brooks/Cole.

Davis, S. R., & Meier, S. T. (2011). Self-monitoring as client self-report and self-intervention. In H. Rosenthal (Ed.), *Favorite counseling and therapy homework assignments* (pp. 115–117). New York: Routledge.

deShazer, S. (1982). *Patterns of brief family therapy.* New York: Guilford.

Diener, M. J., Hilsenroth, M. J., & Weinberger, J. (2007). Therapist affect focus and patient outcomes in psychodynamic psychotherapy: A meta-analysis. *American Journal of Psychiatry, 164,* 936–941. doi: 10.1176/appi.ajp.164.6.936

Dimaggio, G., & Semerari, A. (2004). Disorganized narratives. In L. E. Angus & J. McLeod (Eds.), *The handbook of narrative and psychotherapy* (pp. 263–282). Thousand Oaks, CA: Sage Publications.

Eells, T. D. (Ed.). (1997). *Handbook of psychotherapy case formulation.* New York: Guilford.

Egan, G. (2001). *The skilled helper: A problem-management and opportunity-development approach to helping* (7th ed.). Pacific Grove, CA: Brooks/Cole.

Egan, G. (2009). *The skilled helper: A problem-management and opportunity development approach to helping* (9th ed.). Pacific Grove: CA: Brooks/Cole.

Elliott, R., & Greenberg, L. S. (2001). Process-experiential psychotherapy. In D. J. Cain & J. Seeman (Eds.), *Humanistic psychotherapies* (pp. 279–306). Washington, DC: American Psychological Association.

Ellis, A. (1998). *Rational emotive behavior therapy: A therapist's guide.* San Luis Obispo, CA: Impact.

Ellis, B. (1967). Measurement. In P. Edwards (Ed.), *The encyclopedia of philosophy* (Vol. 5, pp. 241–250). New York: Macmillan.

Epston, D. (2009). *Catching up with David Epston: Down under and up over.* Warrington, England: AFT.

Feldman, C. F., Bruner, J., Renderer, B., & Spitzer, S. (1990). Narrative comprehension. In B. K. Britton & A. D. Pellegrini (Eds.), *Narrative thought and narrative language* (pp. 1–78). Hillsdale, NJ: Erlbaum.

Foa, E., & Jaycox, L. (1999). Cognitive-behavioral theory and treatment of post-traumatic stress disorder. In D. Spiegel (Ed.), *Efficacy and cost-effectiveness of psychotherapy* (pp. 23–61). Arlington, VA: American Psychiatric Publishing.

Foa, E., & Kozak, M. (1986). Emotional processing of fear: Exposure to corrective information. *Psychological Bulletin, 99,* 20–35.

Foa, E., & Riggs, D. (1993). Post-traumatic stress disorder in rape victims. In J. Oldham, M. B. Riba, & A. Tasman (Eds.), *American Psychiatric Press review of psychiatry* (Vol. 12, pp. 273–303). Washington, DC: American Psychiatric Press.

Foa, E. B., Molnar, C., & Cashman, L. (1995). Change in rape narratives during exposure therapy for posttraumatic stress disorder. *Journal of Traumatic Stress, 8,* 675–690. doi: 10.1007/BF02102894

Forbes, R. J., & Dijksterhuis, E. J. (1963). *A history of science and technology* (Vol. 1). Baltimore, MD: Penguin Books.

Frankl, V. (2000). *Man's search for meaning* (3rd ed.). New York: Washington Square Press.

Freedman, J., & Combs, G. (1996). *Narrative therapy.* New York: W.W. Norton.

Fresco, D. M., Frankel, A. N., Mennin, D. S., Turk, C. L., & Heimberg, R. G. (2002). Distinct and overlapping features of rumination and worry: The relationship of cognitive production to negative affective states. *Cognitive Therapy and Research, 26,* 179–188.

Frijda, N. H. (1986). *The emotions.* Cambridge, England: Cambridge University Press.

Geary, J. (2011). *I is an other: The secret life of metaphor and how it shapes the way we see the world.* New York: Harper.

Gergen, K. J. (2001). Psychological science in a postmodern context. *American Psychologist, 56,* 803–813. doi: 10.1037//0003-066X.56.10.803

Glesne, C. (2011). *Become qualitative researchers* (4th ed.). New York: Pearson.

Goldenberg, I., & Goldenberg, H. (1995). Family therapy. In R. J. Corsini & D. Wedding (Eds.), *Current psychotherapies* (5th ed., pp. 356–385). Itasca, IL: Peacock Publishers.

Goldfried, M. (1979) Anxiety reduction through cognitive-behavioral intervention. In P. C. Kendall & S. P. Hollon (Eds.), *Cognitive-behavioral interventions: Theory, research, and procedures* (pp. 65–77). New York: Academic Press.

Goldman, R. N. (1997). *Theme-related depth of experiencing and change in experiential psychotherapy with depressed clients*. Unpublished doctoral dissertation, York University, Toronto, Canada.

Goldstein, M. J., & Palmer, J. O. (1975). *The experience of anxiety: A casebook* (2nd ed.). New York: Oxford University Press.

Gonzalez, D. M. (2001). Client variables and psychotherapy outcomes. In D. J. Cain & J. Seeman (Eds.), *Humanistic psychotherapies* (pp. 559–579). Washington, DC: American Psychological Association.

Goodell, J. (2011). *Shade it black*. Philadelphia: Casemate.

Gordon, D. (1978). *Therapeutic metaphors*. Cupertino, CA: Meta Publications.

Gottman, J. M., & Leiblum, S. R. (1974). *How to do psychotherapy and how to evaluate it*. New York: Holt, Rinehart and Winston.

Gray, G. V., & Lambert, M. J. (2001). Feedback: A key to improving therapy outcomes. *Behavioral Healthcare Tomorrow, 10*, 25–45.

Greenberg, L. S. (2002). *Emotion-focused therapy: Coaching clients to work through their feelings*. Washington, DC: American Psychological Association.

Greenberg, L. S., & Angus, L. E. (2004). The contributions of emotion processes to narrative chance in psychotherapy: A dialectical constructivist approach. In L. E. Angus & J. McLeod (Eds.), *The handbook of narrative and psychotherapy* (pp. 331–364). Thousand Oaks, CA: Sage Publications.

Greenberg, L. S., Korman, L. M., & Paivio, S. C. (2001). Emotion in humanistic psychotherapy. In D. J. Cain & J. Seeman (Eds.), *Humanistic psychotherapies* (pp. 499–530). Washington, DC: American Psychological Association.

Greenberg, L. S., & Safran, J. D. (1984). Integrating affect and cognition: A perspective on the process of therapeutic change. *Cognitive Therapy and Research, 8*, 559–578. doi: 10.1007/BF01173254

Grice, P. (1991). *Studies in the way of words*. Cambridge, MA: Harvard University Press.

Guyker, W. (2006). *Bridging case conceptualization and assessment*. Unpublished manuscript, University at Buffalo, State University of New York.

Habermas, T., Meier, M., & Mukhtar, B. (2009). Are specific emotions narrated differently? *Emotion, 9*, 751–762.

Hager, D. L. (1992). Chaos and growth. *Psychotherapy: Theory, Research, Practice, Training, 29*, 378–384. doi: 10.1037/h0088539

Hardtke, K. K., & Angus, L. E. (2004). The narrative assessment interview. In L. E. Angus & J. McLeod (Eds.), *The handbook of narrative and psychotherapy* (pp. 247–262). Thousand Oaks, CA: Sage Publications.

Hardy, R. E. (1991). *Gestalt psychotherapy*. Springfield, IL: Charles C. Thomas.

Harmon, C., Hawkins, E. J., Lambert, M. J., Slade, K., & Whipple, J. S. (2005). Improving outcomes for poorly responding clients: The use of clinical support tools and feedback to clients. *Journal of Clinical Psychology, 61*, 175–185. doi: 10.1002/jclp.20109

Hayes, A. M., & Strauss, J. L. (1998). Dynamic systems theory as a paradigm for the study of change in psychotherapy: An application of cognitive therapy for depression. *Journal of Consulting and Clinical Psychology, 66*, 939–947. doi: 10.1037//0022-006X.66.6.939

Haywood, H. C., Brown, A. L., & Wingenfeld, S. (1990). Dynamic approaches to psychoeducational assessment. *School Psychology Review, 19*, 411–422.

Heppner, P. P., Cooper, C., Mulholland, A., & Wei, M. (2001). A brief, multidimensional, problem-solving psychotherapy outcome measure. *Journal of Counseling Psychology, 48*, 330–343. doi: 10.1037//0022-0167.48.3.330

Hesketh, B., Pryor, R., & Gleitzman, M. (1989). Fuzzy logic: Toward measuring Gottfredson's concept of occupational social space. *Journal of Counseling Psychology, 36*, 103–109.

Hill, C. E. (1982). Counseling process research: Philosophical and methodological dilemmas. *The Counseling Psychologist, 10*, 7–19. doi: 10.1177/0011000082104003

Hill, C. E. (2004). *Helping skills: Facilitating exploration, insight, and action* (2nd ed.). Washington, DC: American Psychological Association.

Hill, C. E., & O'Brien, K. M. (1999). *Helping skills*. Washington, DC: American Psychological Association.

Hill, C. E., Thompson, B., Cogar, M., & Denman, D. (1993). Beneath the surface of long-term therapy: Therapist and client report of their own and each other's covert processes. *Journal of Counseling Psychology, 40*, 278–288. doi: 10.1037//0022-0167.40.3.278

Hirscheimer, K. (1996). *Development and verification of a measure of unfinished business*. Unpublished master's thesis, Department of Psychology, York University, Toronto, Canada.

Holzer, M., Mergenthaler, E., Pokorny, D., Kachele, H., & Luborsky, L. (1996). Vocabulary measures for the evaluation of therapy outcome: Re-studying transcripts from the Penn Psychotherapy Project. *Psychotherapy Research, 6*, 95–108.

Howard, K. I., Moras, K., Brill, P. L., Martinovich, Z., & Lutz, W. (1996). Evaluation of psychotherapy: Efficacy, effectiveness, and patient progress. *American Psychologist, 51*, 1059–1064. doi: 10.1037//0003-066X.51.10.1059

Huler, S. (2004). *Defining the wind*. New York: Crown.

Hutchby, I. (2005). "Active listening": Formulations and the elicitation of feeling-talk in child counseling. *Research on Language and Social Interaction, 38*, 303–329. doi: 10.1207/s15327973rlsi3803_4

Ivey, A. (2002). *Intentional interviewing and counseling* (4th ed.). Pacific Grove, CA: Brooks/Cole.

Izard, C. E. (2007). Basic emotions, natural kinds, emotion schemas, and a new paradigm. *Perspectives on Psychological Science, 2*, 260–280. doi: 10.1111/j.1745-6916.2007.00044.x

Jankowicz, D. (2003). *Easy guide to repertory grids*. New York: Wiley.

Jongsma, A., & Peterson, L. (1995). *The complete psychotherapy treatment planner*. New York: Wiley.

Judson, H. F. (1980). *The search for solutions*. New York: Holt, Rinehart and Winston.

Kazdin, A. E. (2000). *Psychotherapy for children and adolescents: Directions for research and practice*. New York: Oxford University Press.

Kelly, G. (1955). *The psychology of personal constructs*. New York: Norton.

Kelly, M. A. R., Roberts, J. E., & Ciesla, J. A. (2005). Sudden gains in cognitive behavioral treatment for depression: When do they occur and do they matter? *Behavior Research and Therapy, 43*, 703–714. doi: 10.1016/j.brat.2004.06.002

Kendall, P. C., Hollon, S. D., Beck, A. T., Hammen, C. L., & Ingram, R. E. (1987). Issues and recommendations regarding use of the Beck Depression Inventory. *Cognitive Therapy and Research, 11*, 289–299. doi: 10.1007/BF01186280

Kendall, P. C., Kipnis, D., & Otto-Salaj, L. (1992). When clients don't progress: Influences on and explanations of therapeutic progress. *Cognitive Therapy and Research, 16*, 269–281.

Kensinger, E. A. (2007). Negative emotion enhances memory accuracy: Behavioral and neuroimaging evidence. *Current Directions in Psychological Science, 16*, 213–218. doi: 10.1111/j.1467-8721.2007.00506.x

Kern, J. M. (1991). An evaluation of a novel role-play methodology: The standardized idiographic approach. *Behavior Therapy, 22*, 13–29. doi: 10.1016/S0005-7894(05)80240-0

King, L., Scollon, C., Ramsey, C., & May, T. (2000). Stories of life transition: Subjective well-being and ego development in parents of children with Down Syndrome. *Journal of Research in Personality, 34*, 509–536. doi: 10.1006/jrpe.2000.2285

Klein, M., Mathieu, P., Gendlin, E., & Kiesler, D. (1969). *The experiencing scale*. Madison, WI: Wisconsin Psychiatric Institute.

Klein, M. H., Mathieu-Coughlan, P., & Kiesler, D. J. (1986). The experiencing scales. In L. Greenberg & W. Pinsof (Eds.), *The psychotherapeutic process: A research handbook* (pp. 21–72). New York: Guilford Press.

Kluger, A. N., & DeNisi, A. (1996). Effects of feedback intervention on performance: A historical review, a meta-analysis, and a preliminary feedback intervention theory. *Psychological Bulletin, 119*, 254–284. doi: 10.1037//0033-2909.119.2.254

Kopp, R. R. (1995). *Metaphor therapy: Using client-generated metaphors in psychotherapy*. New York: Brunner-Mazel.

Kopta, S. M., Howard, K. I., Lowry, J. L., & Beutler, L. E. (1994). Patterns of symptomatic recovery in psychotherapy. *Journal of Consulting & Clinical Psychology, 62*, 1009–1016. doi: 10.1037//0022-006X.62.5.1009

Kopta, S. M., & Lowry, J. L. (2002). Psychometric evaluation of the Behavioral Health Questionnaire-20: A brief instrument for assessing global mental health and the three phases of psychotherapy outcome. *Psychotherapy Research, 12*, 413–426.

Kovecses, Z. (2002). *Metaphor: A practical introduction*. New York: Oxford University Press.

Kozak, A. (1992). The epistemic consequences of pervasive and embodied metaphor: Applications to psychotherapy. *Theoretical and Philosophical Psychology, 12*, 137–154. doi: 10.1037/h0091121

Krumboltz, J., & Thoresen, C. (Eds.). (1976). *Counseling methods*. New York: Holt, Rinehart & Winston.

Kuhn, T. S. (1970). *The structure of scientific revolutions*. Chicago, IL: University of Chicago Press.

L'Abate, L. (2011). Psychotherapy consists of homework assignments: Less talk and more interaction—A radical iconoclastic conviction. In H. Rosenthal (Ed.), *Favorite counseling and therapy homework assignments* (pp. 219–229). New York: Routledge.

Lafrance, M. N., & Stoppard, J. M. (2007). Re-storying women's depression: A material-discursive approach. In C. Brown & T. Augusta-Scott (Eds.), *Narrative therapy* (pp. 23–37). Thousand Oaks, CA: Sage Publications.

Lakoff, G., & Johnson, M. (1980). *Metaphors we live by*. Chicago, IL: University of Chicago Press.

Lambert, M. J. (1994). Use of psychological tests for outcome assessment. In M. E. Maruish (Ed.), *The use of psychological testing for treatment planning and outcome assessment* (pp. 75–97). Hillsdale, NJ: Lawrence Erlbaum.

Lambert, M. J. (2001). Psychotherapy outcome and quality improvement: Introduction to the special section on patient-focused research. *Journal of Consulting and Clinical Psychology, 69*, 147–149. doi: 10.1037//0022-006X.69.2.147

Lambert, M. J. (2005). Early response in psychotherapy: Further evidence for the importance of common factors rather than "placebo effects." *Journal of Clinical Psychology, 61*, 855–869. doi: 10.1002/jclp.20130

Lambert, M. J., Garfield, S. L., & Bergin, A. E. (2004). Overview, trends, and future issues. In M. J. Lambert (Ed.), *Bergin and Garfield's handbook of psychotherapy and behavior change* (5th ed., pp. 805–821). New York: Wiley.

Lambert, M. J., Harmon, C., Slade, K., Whipple, J. L., & Hawkins, E. J. (2005). Providing feedback to psychotherapists on their patients' progress: Clinical results and practice suggestions. *Journal of Clinical Psychology, 61*, 165–174. doi: 10.1002/jclp.20113

Lambert, M. J., Hatch, D. R., Kingston, M. D., & Edwards, B. C. (1986). Zung, Beck, and Hamilton Rating Scales as measures of treatment outcome: A meta-analytic comparison. *Journal of Consulting and Clinical Psychology, 54*, 54–59. doi: 10.1037/0022-006X.54.1.54

Lambert, M. J., Whipple, J. L., Smart, D. W., Vermeesch, D. A., Nielsen, S. L., & Hawkins, E. J. (2001). The effects of providing therapists with feedback on patient progress during psychotherapy: Are outcomes enhanced? *Psychotherapy Research, 11*, 49–68. doi: 10.1080/713663852

Lamiell, J. T. (1990). Explanation in the psychology of personality. *Annals of Theoretical Psychology, 6*, 153–192.

Lang, P. J., Cuthbert, B. N., & Bradley, M. M. (1998). Measuring emotion in therapy: Imagery, activation and feeling. *Behavior Therapy, 29*, 655–674. doi: 10.1016/S0005-7894(98)80024-5

Layden, M., Newman, C., Freeman, A., & Morse, S. (1993). *Cognitive therapy of borderline personality disorder*. Needham Heights, MA: Allyn & Bacon.

Lee, J. (1997). Women re-authoring their lives through feminist narrative therapy. *Women & Therapy, 20*, 1–22. doi: 10.1300/J015v20n03_01

Levitt, H. (2002). Voicing the unvoiced: Narrative formulation and silences. *Journal of Counseling Psychology Quarterly, 15*, 333–350.

Levitt, H., Korman, Y., & Angus, L. (2000). A metaphor analysis in treatments of depression: Metaphor as a marker of change. *Counselling Psychology Quarterly, 13*, 23–35.

Levitt, H. M., & Rennie, D. L. (2004). Narrative activity. In L. E. Angus & J. McLeod (Eds.), *The handbook of narrative and psychotherapy* (pp. 299–313). Thousand Oaks, CA: Sage Publications.

Lewin, K. (1935). *A dynamic theory of personality*. New York: McGraw-Hill.

Linehan, M. (1993). *Cognitive behavioral treatment of borderline personality disorder*. New York: Guilford.

Lockhead, G. R. (1992). Psychophysical scaling: Judgments of attributes or objects? *Behavioral and Brain Sciences, 15*, 543–558.

Lockhead, G. R. (1995). Context defines psychology. In F. Kessel (Ed.), *Psychology, science, and human affairs: Essays in honor of William Bevan* (pp. 125–137). Boulder, CO: Westview Press.

Madigan, S. (2011). *Narrative therapy*. Washington, DC: American Psychological Association.

Madill, A., Widdicombe, S., & Barkham, M. (2001). The potential of conversation analysis for psychotherapy research. *The Counseling Psychologist, 29*, 413–434. doi: 10.1177/0011000001293006

Mahoney, M. (1991). *Human change processes: The scientific foundations of psychotherapy*. New York: Basic Books.

Martin, L. L., & Tesser, A. (1996). Some ruminative thoughts. In R. S. Wyer (Ed.), *Ruminative thoughts: Advances in social cognition* (Vol. 9, pp. 1–47). Hillsdale, NJ: Erlbaum.

Mash, E. J., & Hunsley, J. (1993). Assessment considerations in the identification of failing psychotherapy: Bringing the negatives out of the darkroom. *Psychological Assessment, 5*, 292–301. doi: 10.1037//1040-3590.5.3.292

Matsumoto, D. (2001). Culture and emotion. In D. Matsumoto (Ed.), *The handbook of culture and psychology* (pp. 171–194). New York: Oxford University Press.

McAdams, D. P. (1996). Personality, modernity, and the storied self: A contemporary framework for studying persons. *Psychological Inquiry, 7*, 295–321. doi: 10.1207/s15327965pli0704_1

McCarthy, P. (1982). Differential effects of counselor self-referent responses and counselor status. *Journal of Counseling Psychology, 29*, 125–131. doi: 10. 1037//0022-0167.29.2.125

McCarthy, P., & Betz, N. (1978). Differential effects of self-disclosing versus self-involving counselor statements. *Journal of Counseling Psychology, 25*, 251–256. doi: 10.1037/0022-0167.25.4.251

McElroy, S. L., Hudson, J. I., Pope, H. G., & Keck, P. E. (1991). Kleptomania: Clinical characteristics and associated psychopathology. *Psychological Medicine, 21*, 93–108. doi: 10.1017/S0033291700014690

McFall, R. M., & McDonel, E. C. (1986). The continuing search for units of analysis in psychology: Beyond persons, situations, and their interactions. In R. O. Nelson & S. C. Hayes (Eds.), *Conceptual foundations of behavioral assessment* (pp. 201–241). New York: Guilford.

McLaughlin, K. A., Borkovec, T. D., & Sibrava, N. J. (2007). The effects of worry and rumination on affect states and cognitive activity. *Behavior Therapy, 38*, 23–38. doi: 10.1016/j.beth.2006.03.003

McLeod, J. (1997). *Narrative and psychotherapy*. Thousand Oaks, CA: Sage.

McLeod, J. (2004). Social construction, narrative, and psychotherapy. In L. E. Angus & J. McLeod (Eds.), *The handbook of narrative and psychotherapy* (pp. 351–365). Thousand Oaks, CA: Sage Publications.

Meehl, P. E. (1991). Why summaries of research on psychological theories are often uninterpretable. In R. E. Snow & D. E. Wiley (Eds.), *Improving inquiry in social science* (pp. 13–59). Hillsdale, NJ: Lawrence Erlbaum.

Meier, S. (1987). An unconnected special issue. *American Psychologist, 42*, 881.

Meier, S. (1994). *The chronic crisis in psychological measurement and assessment.* New York: Academic Press.

Meier, S. (2003). *Bridging case conceptualization, assessment, and intervention.* Thousand Oaks, CA: Sage Publications.

Meier, S. (2008a). Narrative therapy. In F. T. Leong, E. Altmaier, M. G. Constantine, H. E. A. Tinsley, & B. Walsh (Eds.), *Encyclopedia of counseling, Vol. 2: Personal and emotional counseling* (pp. 693–695). Thousand Oaks, CA: Sage Publications.

Meier, S. (2008b). *Measuring change in counseling and psychotherapy*. New York: Guilford.

Meier, S. (2011). *The Depression/Anxiety Negative Affect (DANA) Scale—Experimental.* Unpublished manuscript, University at Buffalo.

Meier, S., & Davis, S. (2011). *The elements of counseling* (7th ed.). Pacific Grove, CA: Brooks/Cole.

Meier, S. T. (1999). Training the practitioner-scientist: Bridging case conceptualization, assessment, and intervention. *The Counseling Psychologist, 27*, 846–869. doi: 10.1177/0011000099276008

Meier, S. T., & Schwartz, E. (2007). *Negative changes on new outcome assessments with adolescent clients: A social desirability effect?* Unpublished manuscript, University at Buffalo.

Meier, S. T., & Vermeersch, D. (2007). *What changes in counseling and psychotherapy?* Unpublished manuscript, University at Buffalo.

Mergenthaler, E. (1996). Emotion-abstraction patterns in verbatim protocols: A new way of describing psychotherapeutic processes. *Journal of Consulting and Clinical Psychology, 64*, 1306–1315. doi: 10.1037//0022-006X.64.6.1306

Miles, M. B., & Huberman, A. M. (1990). *Qualitative data analysis*. Thousand Oaks, CA: Sage Publications.

Milliken, C. S., Auchterlonie, J. L., & Hoge, C. W. (2007). Longitudinal assessment of mental health problems among active and reserve component soldiers returning from the Iraq war. *Journal of the American Medical Association, 298*, 2141–2148. doi: 10.1001/jama.298.18.2141

Minuchin, S. (1974). *Families and family therapy*. Cambridge, MA: Harvard University Press.

Mohr, D., Shoham-Solomon, V., Engle, D., & Beutler, L. (1991). The expression of anger in psychotherapy for depression: Its role and measurement. *Psychotherapy Research, 1*, 124–134.

Moses, E. B., & Barlow, D. H. (2006). A new unified treatment approach for emotional disorders based on emotion science. *Current Directions in Psychological Science, 15*, 146–150.

Murray, H. A. (1938). *Explorations in personality*. New York: Oxford University Press.

Needleman, L. D. (1999). *Cognitive case conceptualization*. Mahwah, NJ: Erlbaum.

Neimeyer, G. (Ed.). (1993). *Constructivist assessment: A casebook*. Thousand Oaks, CA: Sage.

Neimeyer, R. (Ed.). (2001). *Meaning reconstruction and the experience of loss*. Washington, DC: American Psychological Association.

Neimeyer, R., & Neimeyer, G. (1993). Constructivist assessment: What and when. In G. Neimeyer (Ed.), *Constructivist assessment: A casebook* (pp. 206–223). Thousand Oaks, CA: Sage.

Nelson, R. O. (1977). Assessment and therapeutic functions of self-monitoring. In M. Hersen, R. M. Eisler, & P. M. Miller (Eds.), *Progress in behavior modification* (Vol. 5, pp. 263–308). New York: Brunner/Mazel.

Nezu, A. M., Ronan, G. F., Meadows, E. A., & McClure, K. S. (2000). *Practitioner's guide to empirically based measures of depression*. New York: Kluwer Academic/Plenum.

Ng, K. S. (1999). *Counseling Asian families from a systems perspective*. Alexandria, VA: American Counseling Association.

Nolen-Hoeksema, S. (1996). Chewing the cud and other ruminations. In R. S. Wyer (Ed.), *Ruminative thoughts* (pp. 135–144). Hillsdale, NJ: Lawrence Erlbaum.

O'Hanlon, W. H. (2009). *A guide to trance land: A practical handbook of Ericksonian and solution-focused hypnosis*. New York: Norton.

Paivio, S. C., & Greenberg, L. S. (1995). Resolving "unfinished business": Efficacy of experiential therapy using empty-chair dialogue. *Journal of Consulting and Clinical Psychology, 63*, 419–425. doi: 10.1037//0022-006X.63.3.419

Parker, I. (2010, November 15). Paths of glory. *The New Yorker*, pp. 54–67.

Paul, G. L. (1967). Strategy of outcome research in psychotherapy. *Journal of Consulting Psychology, 31*, 109–118. doi: 10.1037/h0024436

Paul, G. L. (Ed.). (1986). *Assessment in residential treatment settings*. Champaign, IL: Research Press.

Payne, J. D., & Kensinger, E. A. (2010). Sleep's role in the consolidation of emotional episodic memories. *Current Directions in Psychological Science, 19*, 290–295.

Pennebaker, J. W. (1993). Putting stress into words: Health, linguistic, and therapeutic implications. *Behaviour Research and Therapy, 31*, 539–548.

Pennebaker, J. W., Francis, M., & Booth, R. (2001). *Linguistic inquiry and word count (LIWC): LIWC 2001*. Mahwah, NJ: Erlbaum.

Pennebaker, J. W., Mayne, T. J., & Francis, M. E. (1997). Linguistic predictors of adaptive bereavement. *Journal of Personality and Social Psychology, 72*, 863–871.

Pennebaker, J. W., Mehl, M. R., & Niederhoffer, K. G. (2003). Psychological aspects of natural language use: Our words, our selves. *Annual Review of Psychology, 54*, 547–577.

Pennebaker, J. W., Zech, E., & Rimé, B. (2001). Disclosing and sharing emotion: Psychological, social and health consequences. In M. S. Stroebe, R. O. Hansson, W. Stroebe, & H. Schut (Eds.), *Handbook of bereavement research: Consequences, coping, and care* (pp. 517–544). Washington, DC: American Psychological Association.

Perls, F. (1992). *Gestalt therapy verbatim*. Highland, NY: Gestalt Journal Press.

Perls, F., Hefferline, R. F., & Goodman, P. (1951). *Gestalt therapy*. New York: Dell.

Persons, J. B. (1991). Psychotherapy outcome studies do not accurately represent current models of psychotherapy: A proposed remedy. *American Psychologist, 46*, 99–106. doi: 10.1037//0003-066X.46.2.99

Persons, J. B., & Mikami, A. Y. (2002). Strategies for handling treatment failure successfully. *Psychotherapy: Theory/Research/Practice/Training, 39*, 139–151.

Pierce, R. A., Nichols, M. P., & Dubrin, J. R. (1983). *Emotional expression in psychotherapy*. New York: Gardner Press.

Pistole, M. C. (2003). Dance as metaphor: Complexities and extensions in psychotherapy. *Psychotherapy: Theory, Research, Practice, Training, 40*, 232–241. doi: 10.1037/0033–3204.40.3.232

Polkinghorne, D. E. (2004). Narrative therapy and postmodernism. In L. E. Angus & J. McLeod (Eds.), *The handbook of narrative and psychotherapy* (pp. 53–67). Thousand Oaks, CA: Sage Publications.

Progoff, I. (1992). *At a journal workshop*. New York: Tarcher.

Rae, J. (2008). Lexical substitution as a therapeutic resource. In A. Perakyla, C. Antaki, S. Vehvilainen, & I. Leudar (Eds.), *Conversation analysis and psychotherapy*. Cambridge, UK: Cambridge University Press.

Rasmussen, B., & Angus, L. (1996). Metaphor in psychodynamic psychotherapy with borderline and non-borderline clients: A qualitative analysis. *Psychotherapy: Theory, Research, Practice, Training, 33*, 521–530. doi: 10.1037/0033-3204.33.4.521

Ridley, C. R., Li, L. C., & Hill, C. L. (1998). Multicultural assessment: Reexamination, reconceptualization, and practical application. *The Counseling Psychologist, 26*, 827–910. doi: 10.1177/0011000098266001

Ronnestad, M. H., & Skovholt, T. M. (2003). The journey of the counselor and therapist: Research findings and perspectives on professional development. *Journal of Career Development, 30*, 5–44. doi: 10.1177/089484530303000102

Rosenthal, H. (Ed.). (2011) *Favorite counseling and therapy homework assignments*. New York: Routledge.

Rotter, J. (1966). Generalized expectancies of internal versus external control of reinforcements. *Psychological Monographs, 80* (1, Whole No. 609).

Samoilov, A., & Goldfried, M. R. (2000). Role of emotion in cognitive-behavior therapy. *Clinical Psychology: Science and Practice, 7*, 373–385. doi: 10.1093/clipsy.7.4.373

Sapyta, J. (2004). *The effect of the provision of information on client status toward clinician behavior and outcome: A meta-analysis*. Manuscript submitted for publication.

Sapyta, J., Riemer, M., & Bickman, L. (2005). Feedback to clinicians: Theory, research, and practice. *Journal of Clinical Psychology, 61*, 145–153. doi: 10.1002/jclp.20107

Satir, V. (1988). *New people-making* (2nd ed.). Palo Alto, CA: Science and Behavior Books.

Schwarz, N. (2010). Measurement as cooperative communication: What research participants learn from questionnaires. In G. Walford, E. Tucker, & M. Viswanathan (Eds.), *The Sage handbook of measurement* (pp. 43–60). Los Angeles: Sage Publications.

Segal, Z., Williams, J., & Teasdale, J. D. (2002). *Mindfulness-based cognitive therapy for depression*. New York: Guilford.

Semmler, P. L., & Braun, C. B. (2000). Narrative therapy: A storied context for multicultural counseling. *Journal of Multicultural Counseling and Development, 28*, 51–62.

Shedler, J., Mayman, M., & Manis, M. (1993). The illusion of mental health. *American Psychologist, 48*, 1117–1131.

Shinn, M. R. (2007). Identifying students at risk, monitoring performance, and determining eligibility within response to intervention: Research on educational need and benefit from academic intervention. *School Psychology Review, 36*, 601–617.

Shostrom, E. L. (Producer). (1965). *Three approaches to psychotherapy.* Santa Ana, CA: Psychological Films.

Sigmon, S. T., Pells, J. J., Boulard, N. E., Whitcomb-Smith, S., Edenfield, T. M., Hermann, B. A., ... Kubik, E. (2005). Gender differences in self-reports of depression: The response bias hypothesis revisited. *Sex Roles, 53*, 401–411. doi: 10.1007/s11199-005-6762-3

Silver, E., Williams, A., Worthington, F., & Phillips, N. (1998). Family therapy and soiling: An audit of externalizing and other approaches. *Journal of Family Therapy, 20*, 413–422. doi: 10.1111/1467-6427.00096

Singer, J. E., & Blagov, P. S. (2004). Self-defining memories, narrative identity, and psychotherapy. In L. E. Angus & J. McLeod (Eds.), *The handbook of narrative and psychotherapy* (pp. 229–246). Thousand Oaks, CA: Sage Publications.

Smith, M. L., & Glass, G. V. (1977). Meta-analysis of psychotherapy outcome studies. *American Psychologist, 32*, 752–760. doi: 10.1037//0003-066X.32.9.752

Smyth, J. M. (1998). Written emotional expression: Effect sizes, outcome types, and moderating variables. *Journal of Consulting and Clinical Psychology, 66*, 174–184. doi: 10.1037//0022-006X.66.1.174

Somova, M., & Meier, S. T. (2009). *Sensitivity to change of the Behavioral Health Questionnaire's (BHQ-20) total and item scores.* Unpublished manuscript, University at Buffalo.

Sommers-Flanagan, J., & Sommers-Flanagan, R. (1999). *Clinical interviewing* (2nd ed.). Boston: Allyn & Bacon.

Speight, S. L., & Vera, E. M. (2001). A social justice agenda: Ready, or not? *The Counseling Psychologist, 32*, 109–118. doi: 10.1177/0011000003260005

Spielberger, C. D., Sydeman, S., Owen, A. E., & Marsh, B. J. (1997). Measuring anxiety and anger with the State-Trait Anxiety Inventory (STAI) and State-Trait Anger Expression Inventory (STAXI). In M. Maruish (Ed.), *The use of psychological testing for treatment planning and outcome assessment* (2nd ed., pp. 993–1022). Mahwah, NJ: Erlbaum.

Stiles, W. B. (2001). Future directions in research on humanistic psychotherapy. In D. J. Cain & J. Seeman (Eds.), *Humanistic psychotherapies* (pp. 605–616). Washington, DC: American Psychological Association.

Stiles, W. B. (2002). Assimilation of problematic experiences. In J. Norcross (Ed.), *Psychotherapy relationships that work: Therapist contributions and responsiveness to patients* (pp. 357–365). New York: Oxford University Press.

Stott, R., Mansell, W., Salkovskis, P., Lavender, A., & Cartwright-Hatton, S. (2010). *Oxford guide to metaphors in CBT*. Oxford, UK: Oxford University Press.

Strauss, A., & Corbin, J. (Eds.). (1997). *Grounded theory in practice*. Thousand Oaks, CA: Sage Publications.

Tausczik, Y. R., & Pennebaker, J. W. (2010). The psychological meaning of words: LIWC and computerized text analysis methods. *Journal of Language and Social Psychology, 29*, 24–54. doi: 10.1177/0261927X09351676

Tedeschi, R. G., & Calhoun, L. G. (2004). Posttraumatic growth: Conceptual foundations and empirical evidence. *Psychological Inquiry, 15*, 1–18. doi: 10.1207/s15327965pli1501_01

Teyber, E., & McClure, F. (2011). *Interpersonal process in psychotherapy* (6th ed.). Pacific Grove, CA: Brooks/Cole.

Tryon, W. W. (1991). *Activity measurement in psychology and medicine*. New York: Plenum.

Tull, M. T., & Roemer, L. (2007). Emotion regulation difficulties associated with the experience of uncued panic attacks: Evidence of experiential avoidance, emotional nonacceptance, and decreased emotional clarity. *Behavior Therapy, 38*, 378–391. doi: 10.1016/j.beth.2006.10.006

Vermeersch, D. A., Lambert, M. J., & Burlingame, G. M. (2000). Outcome questionnaire: Item sensitivity to change. *Journal of Personality Assessment, 74*, 242–261. doi: 10.1207/S15327752JPA7402_6

Vermeersch, D. A., Whipple, J. L., Lambert, M. J., Hawkins, E. J., Burchfield, C. M., & Okiishi, J. C. (2004). Outcome questionnaire: Is it sensitive to changes in counseling center clients? *Journal of Counseling Psychology, 51*, 38–49. doi: 10.1037/0022-0167.51.1.38

Viney, L. (1993). *Life stories: Personal construct therapy for the elderly*. Chichester, UK: Wiley.

Voogt, E., Van Der Heide, A., Van Leeuwen, A. F., Visser, A. P., Cleiren, M., Passchier, J., & Van Der Maas, P. J. (2005). Positive and negative affect after diagnosis of advanced cancer. *Psycho-Oncology, 14*, 262–273.

Vromans, L. P., & Schweitzer, R. D. (2010). Narrative therapy for adults with a major depressive disorder: Improved symptom and interpersonal outcomes. *Psychotherapy Research, 21*, 4–15.

Wachtel, P. L. (1973). Psychodynamics, behavior therapy, and the implacable experimenter: An inquiry into the consistency of personality. *Journal of Abnormal Psychology, 82*, 321–334. doi: 10.1037/h0035132

Wallerstein, R. S. (1982). Foreword. In D. Spence (Ed.), *Narrative truth and historical truth*. New York: Norton.

Wampold, B. E. (2001). *The great psychotherapy debate: Models, methods, and findings*. Mahwah, NJ: Erlbaum.

Watkins, C. E., & Schneider, L. J. (1989). Self-involving versus self-disclosing counselor statements during an initial interview. *Journal of Counseling and Development, 67*, 345–349.

Watkins, E., & Moulds, M. (2005). Distinct modes of ruminative self-focus: Impact of abstract versus concrete rumination on problem solving in depression. *Emotions, 5*, 319–328. doi: 10.1037/1528-3542.5.3.319

Watson, D., Clark, L., & Tellegen, A. (1988). Development and validation of brief measures of positive and negative affect: The PANAS scales. *Journal of Personality and Social Psychology, 54*, 1063–1070.

Watson, D., & Kendall, P. C. (1989). Understanding anxiety and depression: Their relation to negative and positive affective states. In P. C. Kendall & D. Watson (Eds.), *Anxiety and depression* (pp. 3–26). San Diego: Academic Press.

Weber, M., Davis, K., & McPhie, L. (2006). Narrative therapy, eating disorders and groups: Enhancing outcomes in rural NSW. *Australian Social Work, 59*, 391–405. doi: 10.1080/03124070600985970

Weg, A. H. (2011). *OCD treatment through storytelling*. Oxford, UK: Oxford University Press.

Weinstock, M., & Meier, S. T. (2003). A comparison of two item selection methodologies for measuring change in university counseling center clients. *Measurement and Evaluation in Counseling & Development, 36*, 66–75.

White, M. (2004). Folk psychology and narrative practices. In L. E. Angus & J. McLeod (Eds.), *The handbook of narrative and psychotherapy* (pp. 15–52). Thousand Oaks, CA: Sage Publications.

White, M., & Epston, D. (1990). *Narrative means to therapeutic ends*. New York: W. W. Norton.

Wickman, S. (2000). "Making something of it": An analysis of the conversation and language of Carl Rogers and Gloria. *Dissertation Abstracts International, 60 (8-B)*, pp. 4260.

Wickman, S. A., & Campbell, C. (2003). The co-construction of congruency: Investigating the conceptual metaphors of Carl Rogers and Gloria. *Counselor Education and Supervision, 43*, 15–24.

Wiger, D. (1999). *The psychotherapy documentation primer*. New York: Wiley.

Young, J. E., Klosko, J. S., & Weishaar, M. E. (2003). *Schema therapy*. New York: Guilford.

Zeig, J. K. (Ed.). (1982). *Ericksonian approaches to hypnosis and psychotherapy.* New York: Brunner/Mazel.

Zhong, C. (2008). Application of proverbs in psychotherapy for the Chinese. *World Cultural Psychiatry Research Review, 3,* 16–19.

Zinn, J. (2006). I'm like, so fat: Helping your teen make healthy choices about eating and exercise in a weight-obsessed world. *Eating Disorders: The Journal of Treatment & Prevention, 14,* 171–172.

Ziskin, J. Z. (1995). *Coping with psychiatric and psychological testimony* (5th ed.). Los Angeles: Law and Psychology Press.

Subject Index

Dialogues Index

Note: Client themes about negative affect (NA) are in italics while avoidance themes are underlined.

Client Themes Index

Note: Client themes about negative affect (NA) are in italics.

Therapist Responses Index